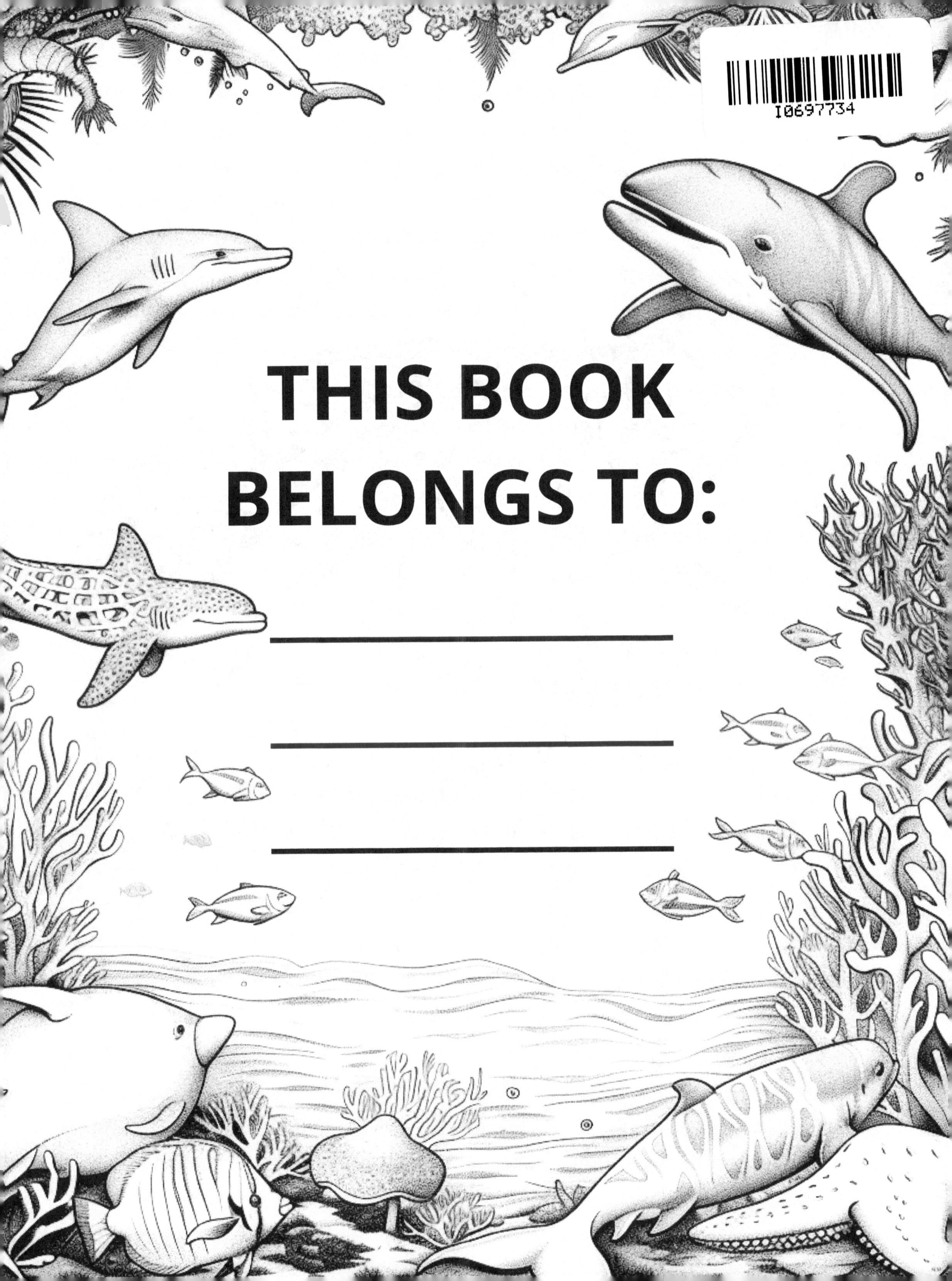

THIS BOOK
BELONGS TO:

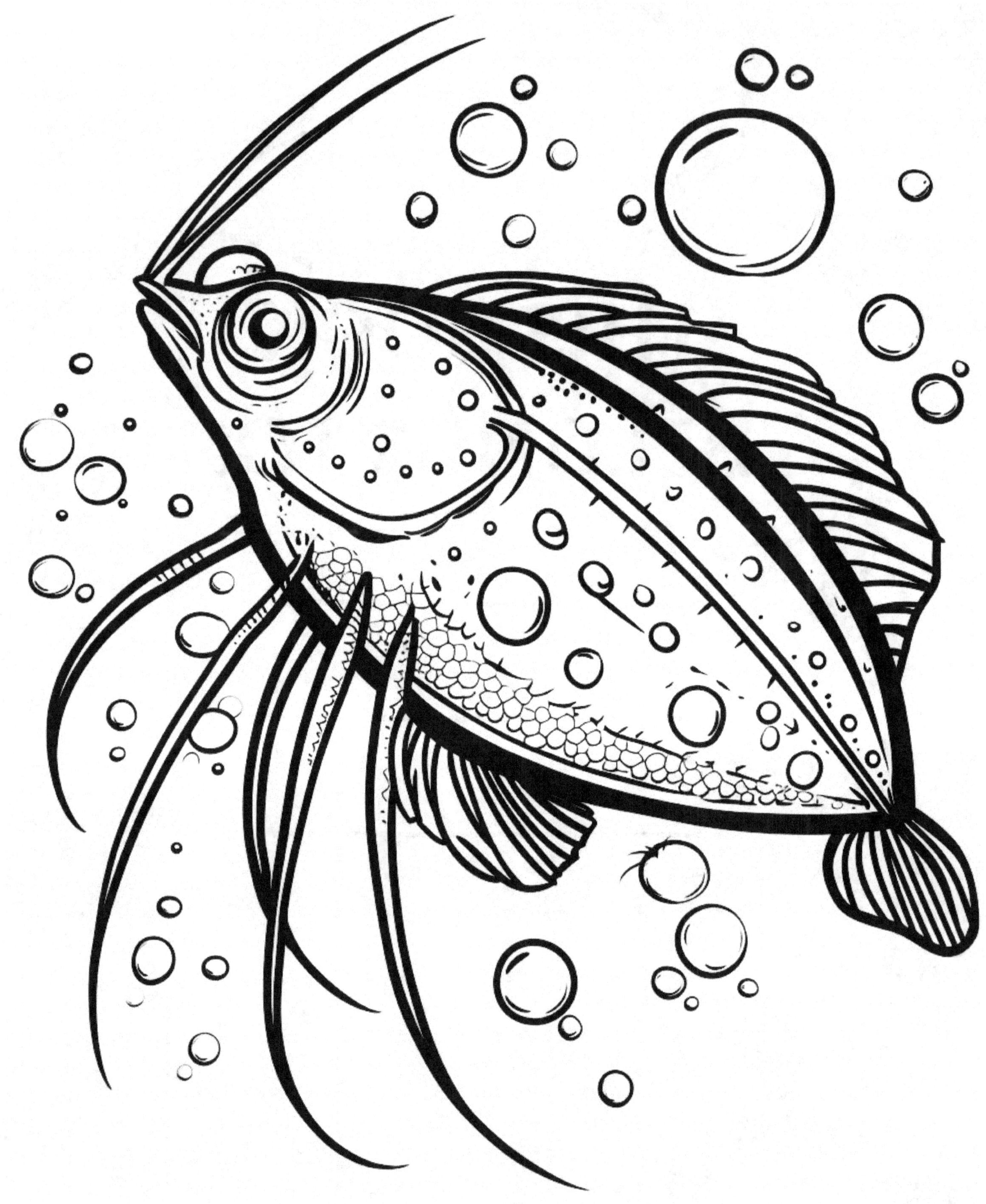

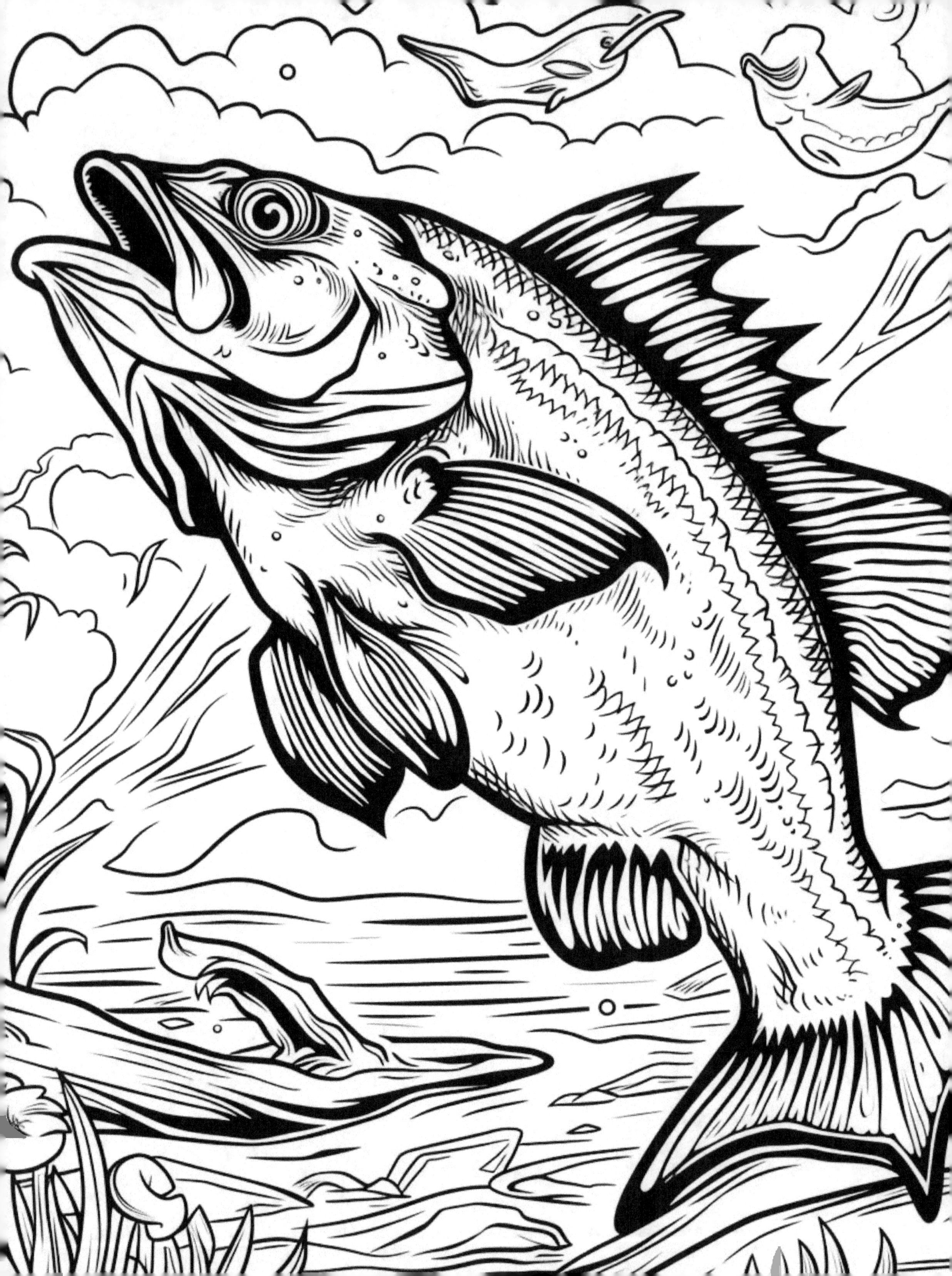

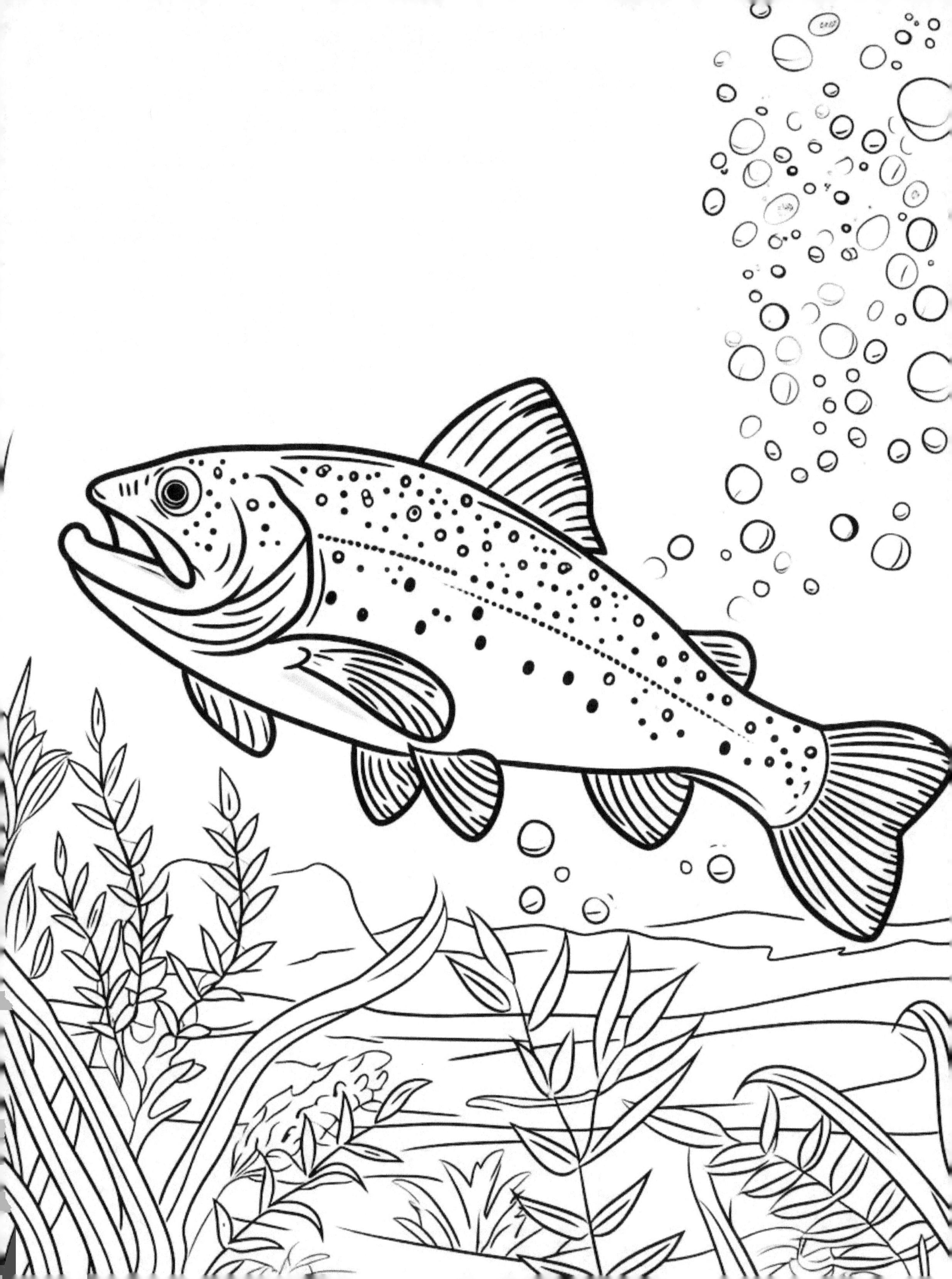

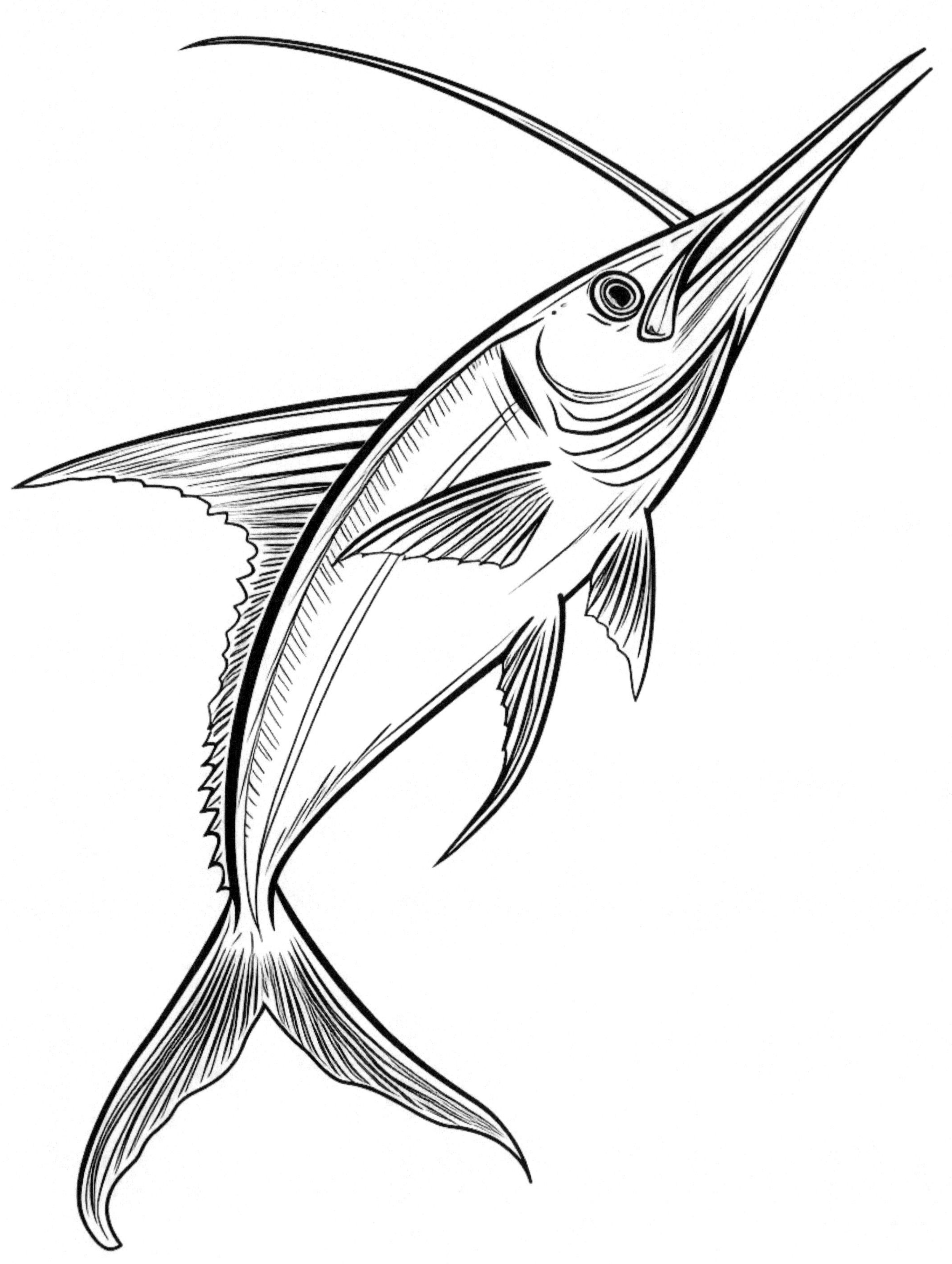

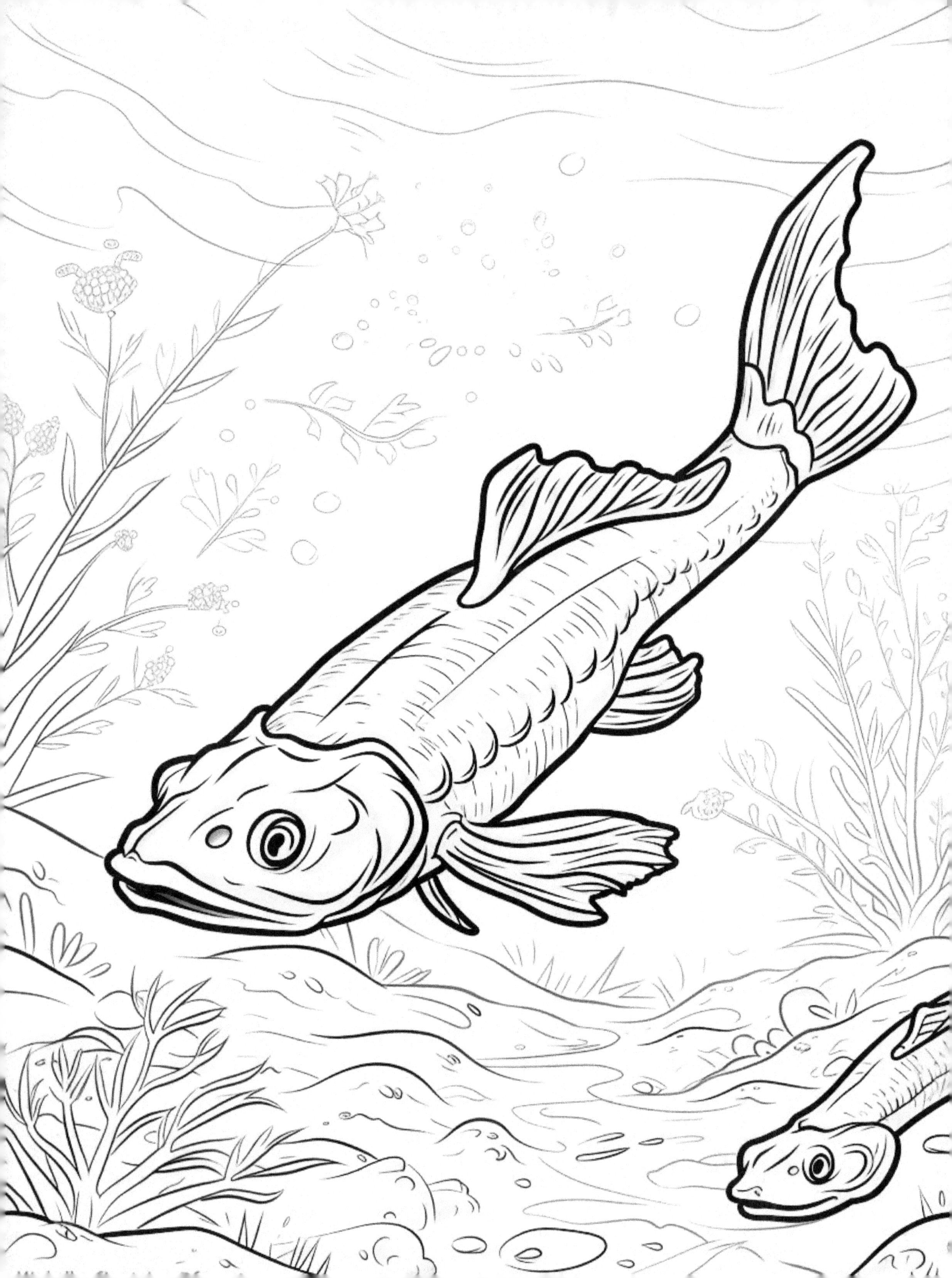

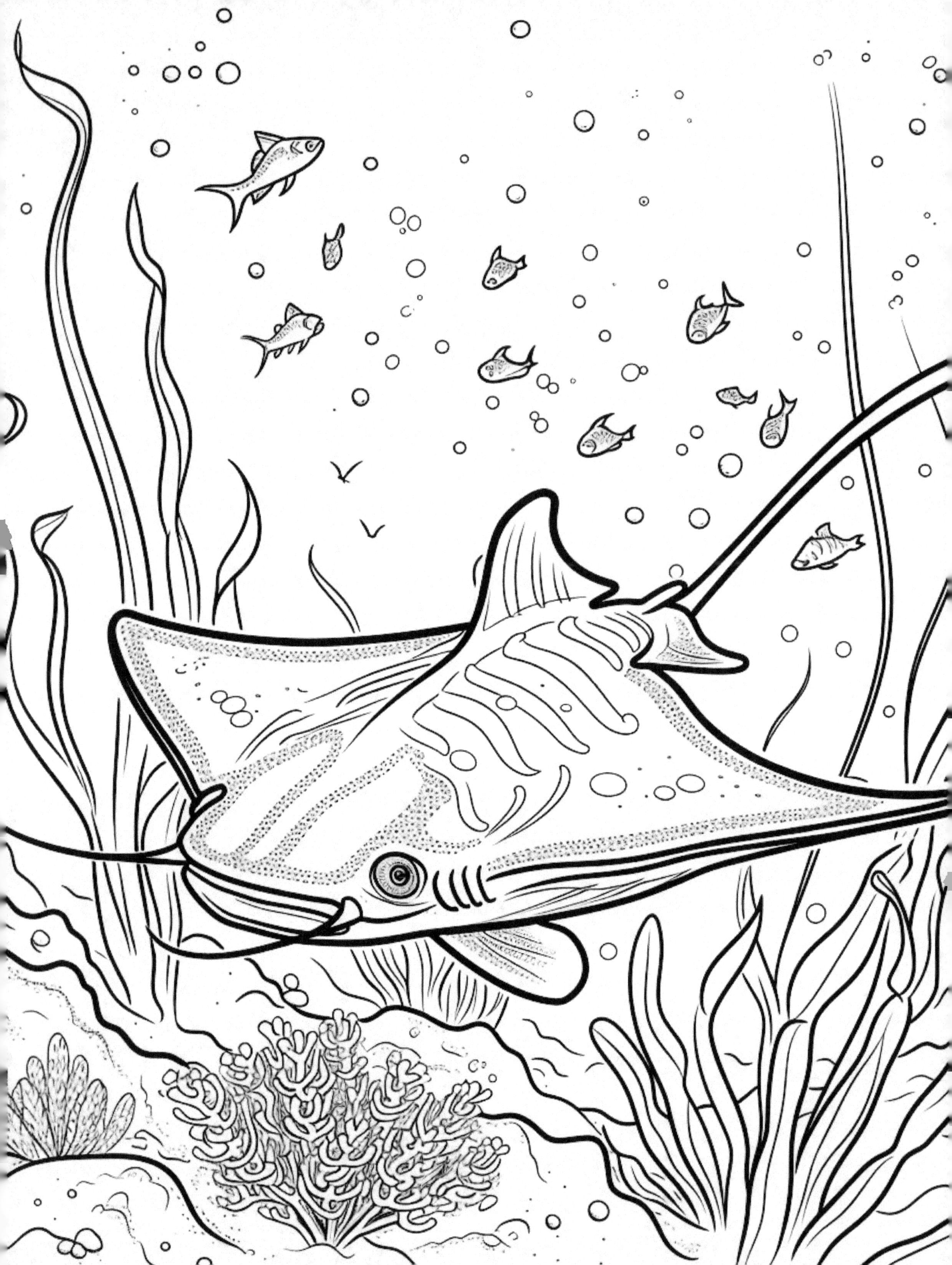

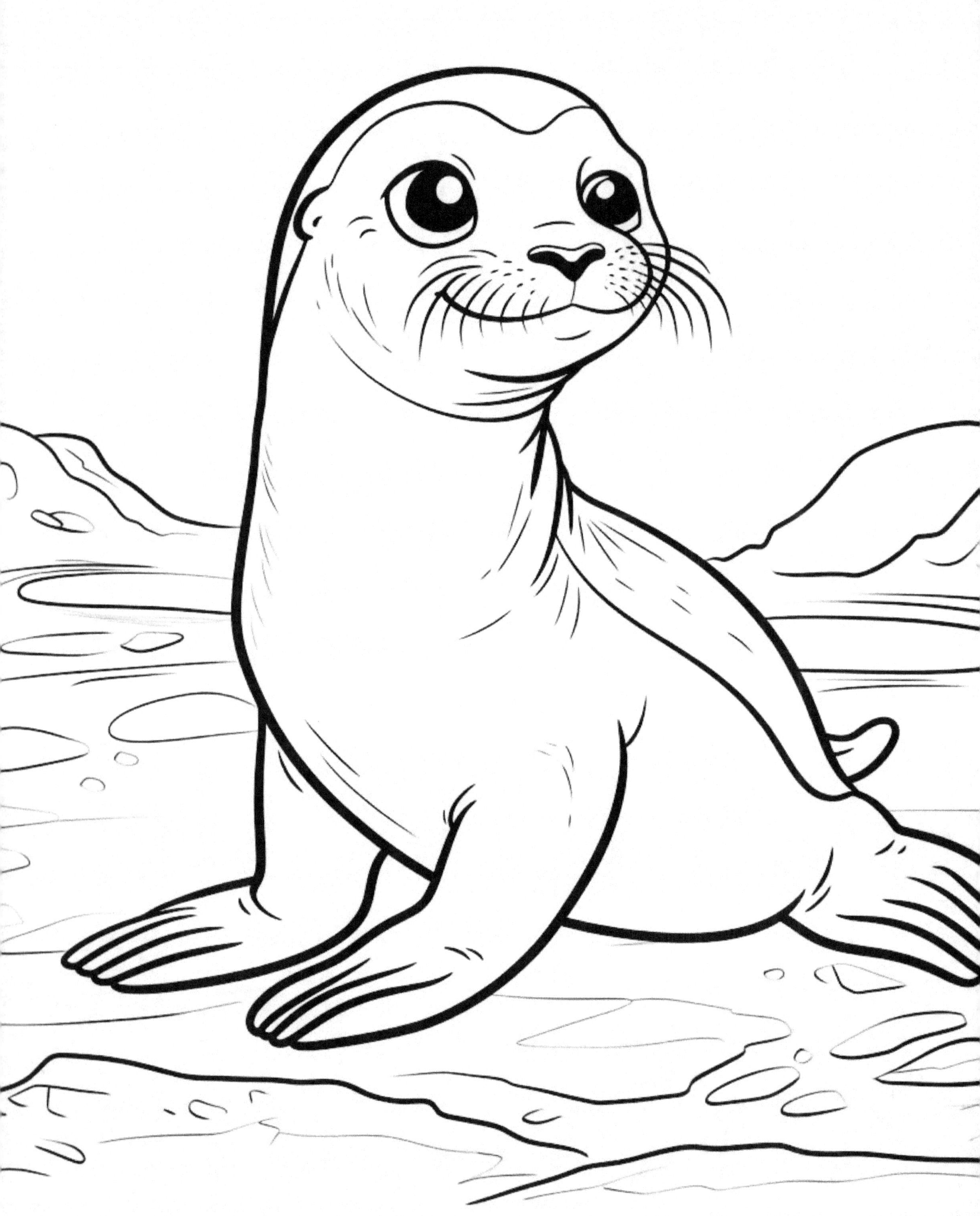

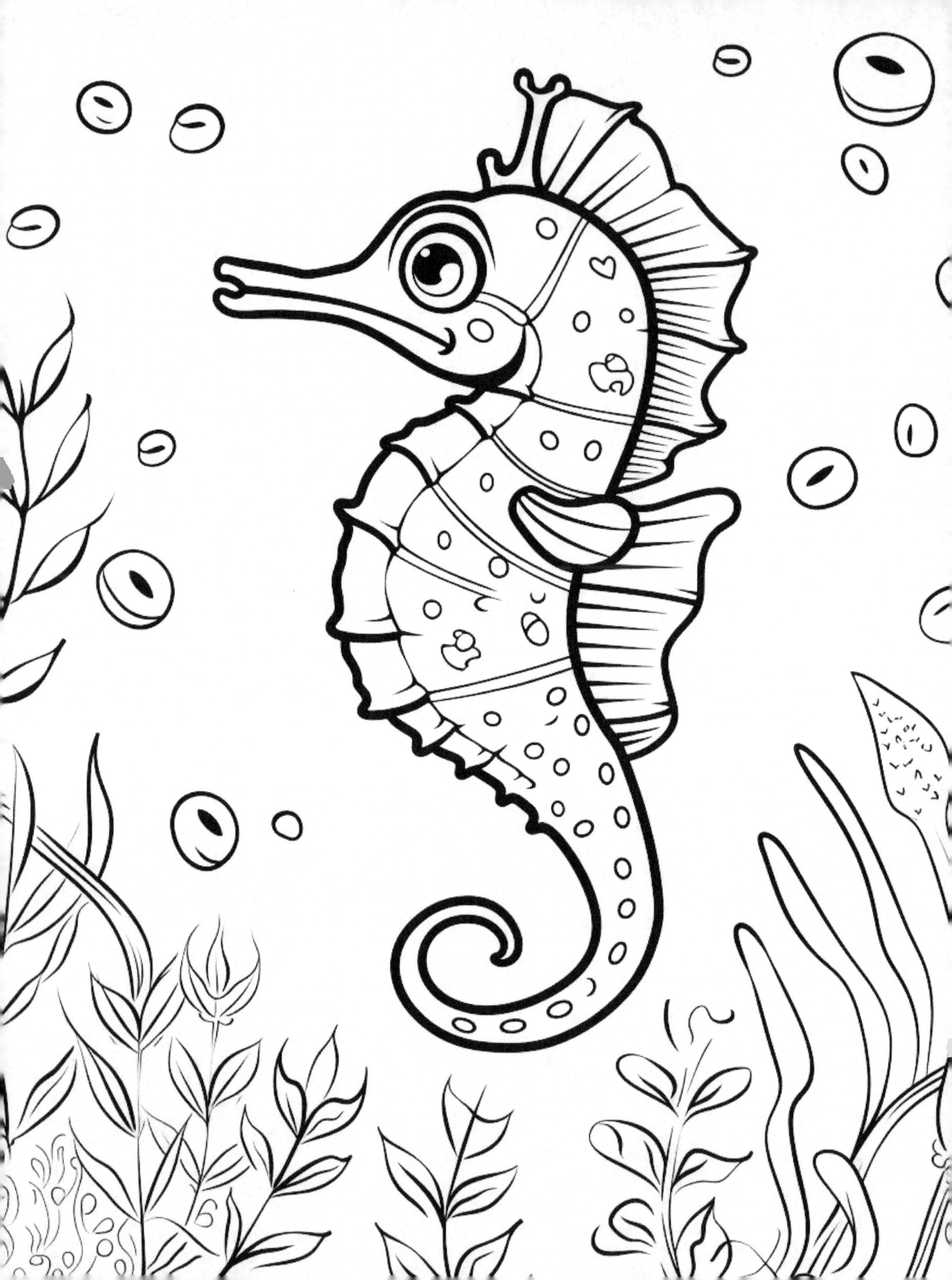

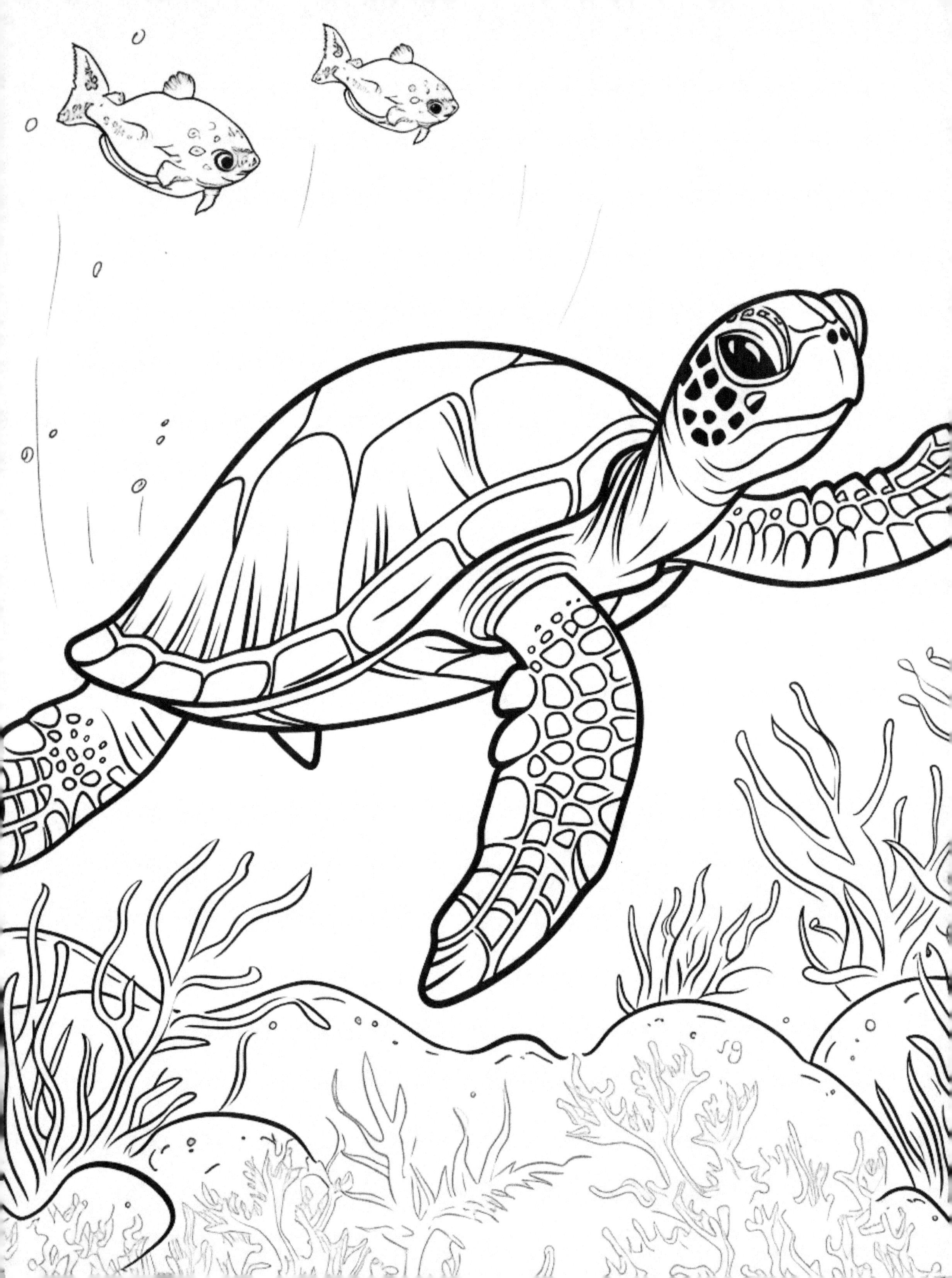

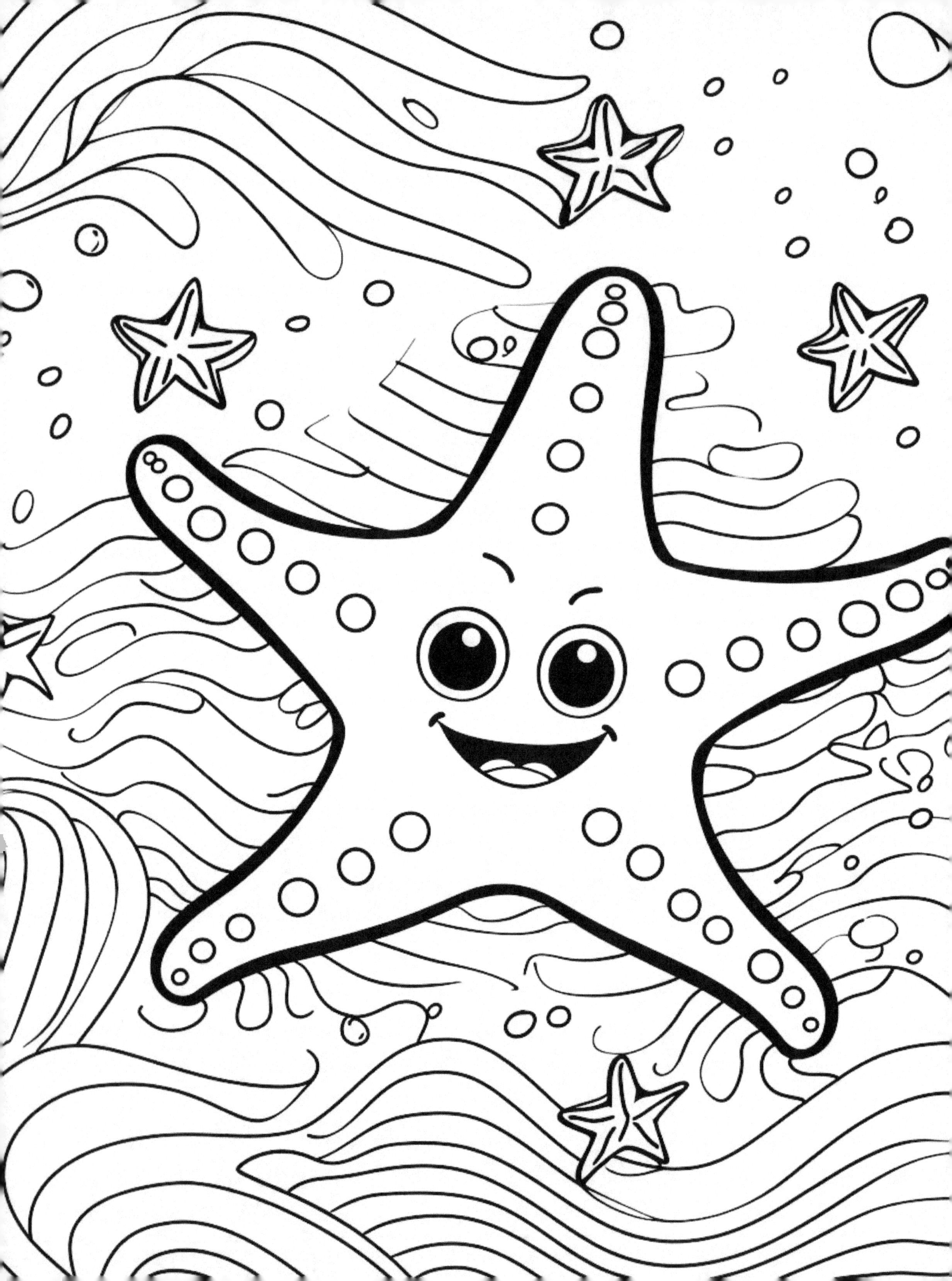

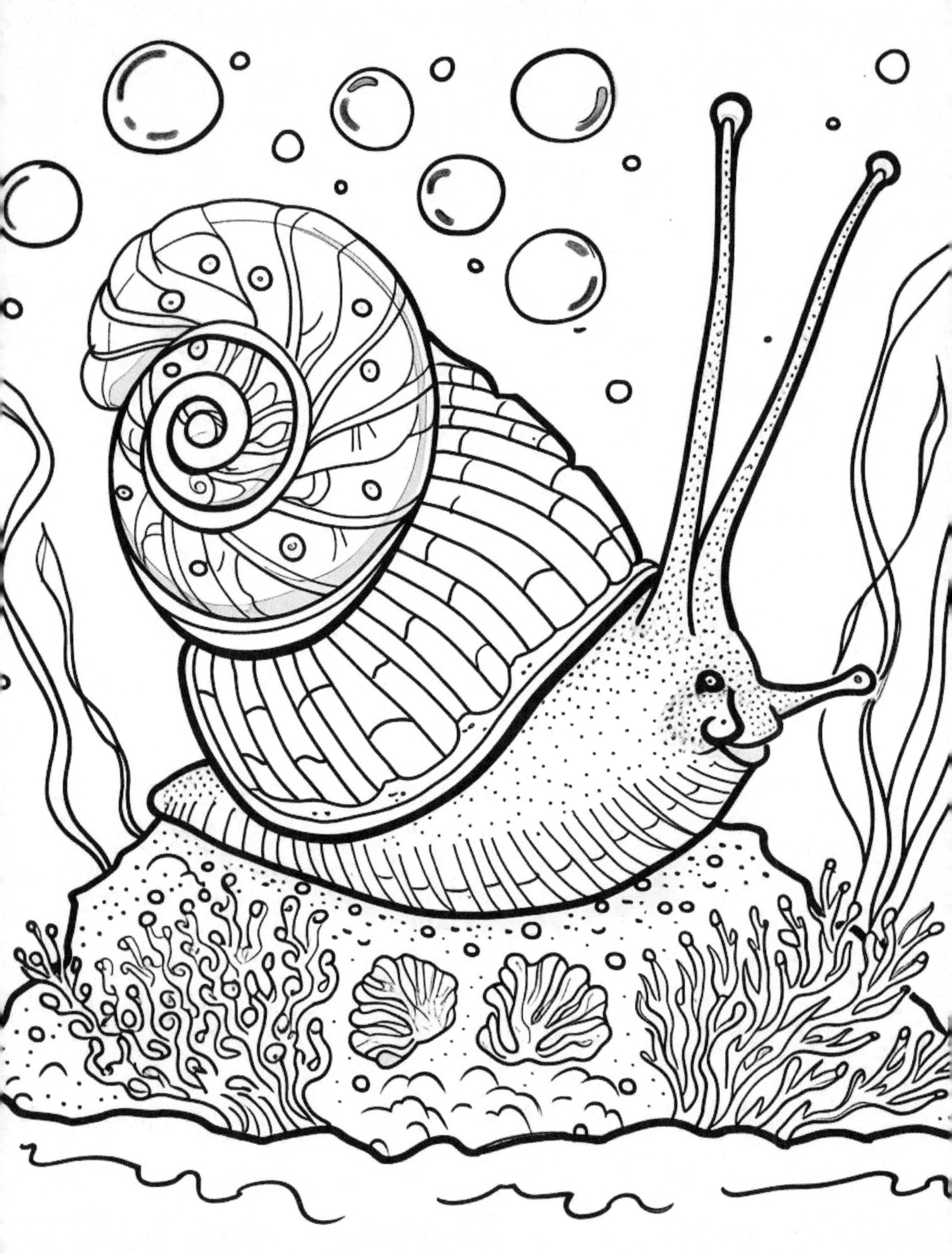

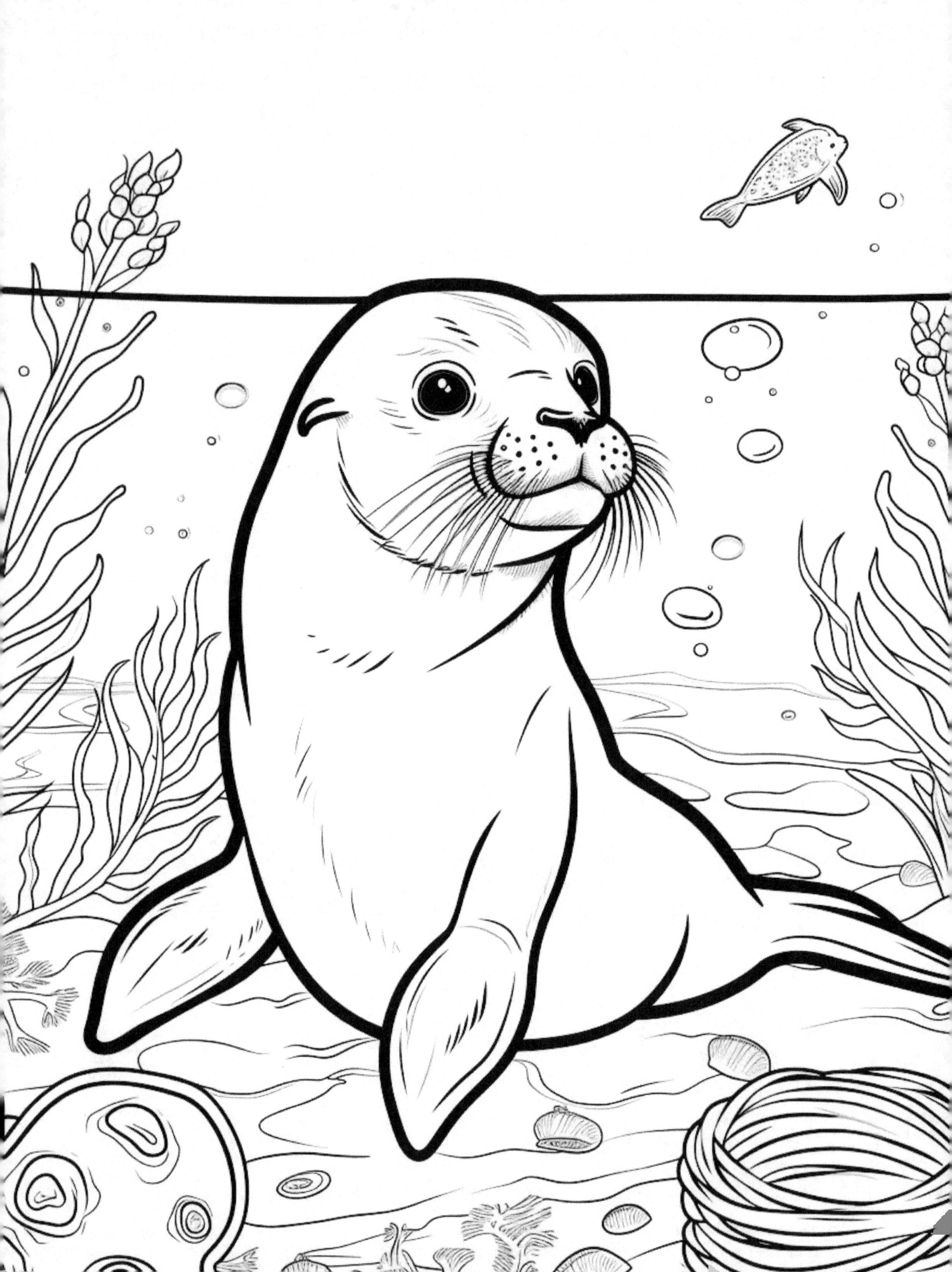

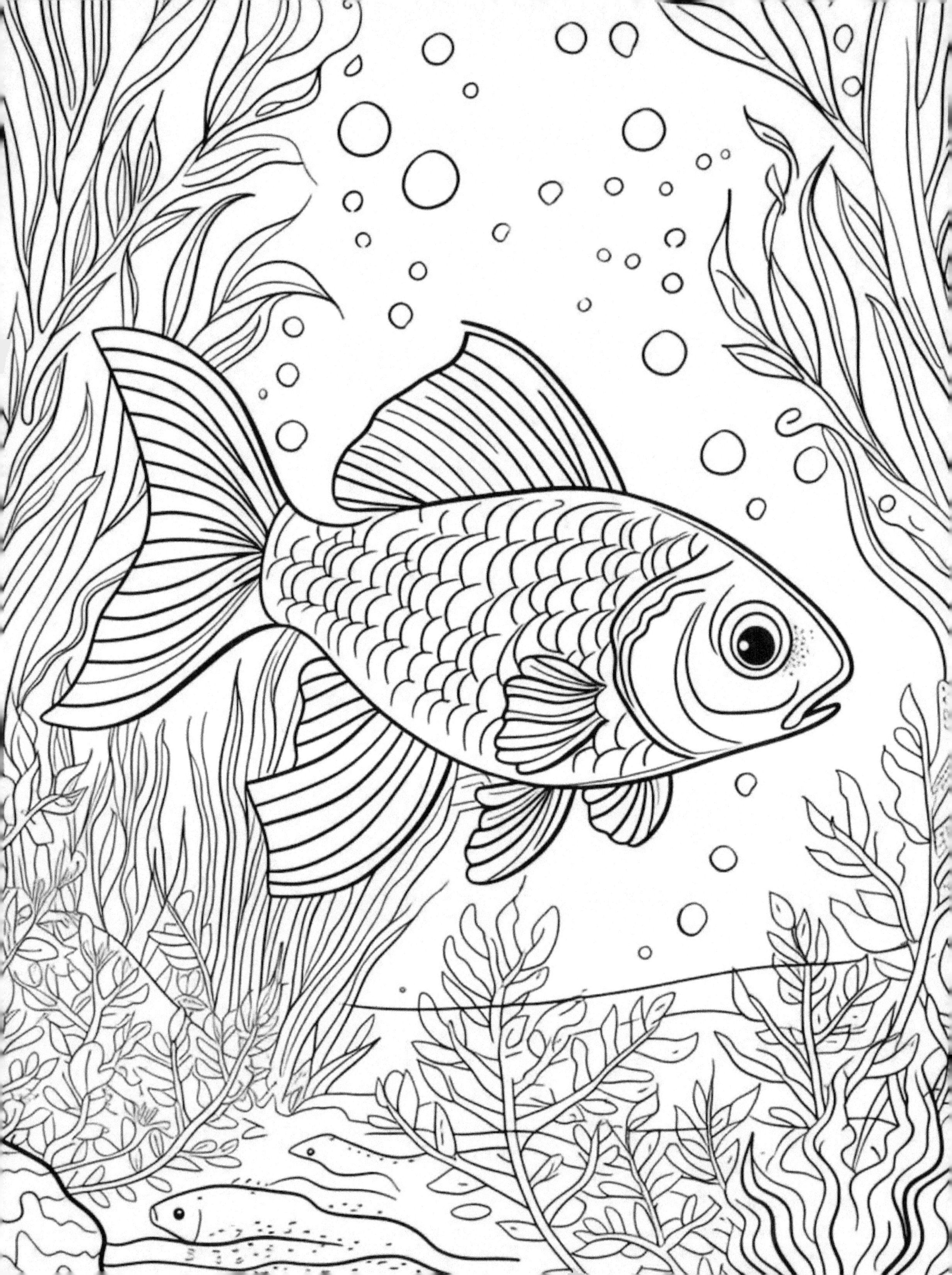

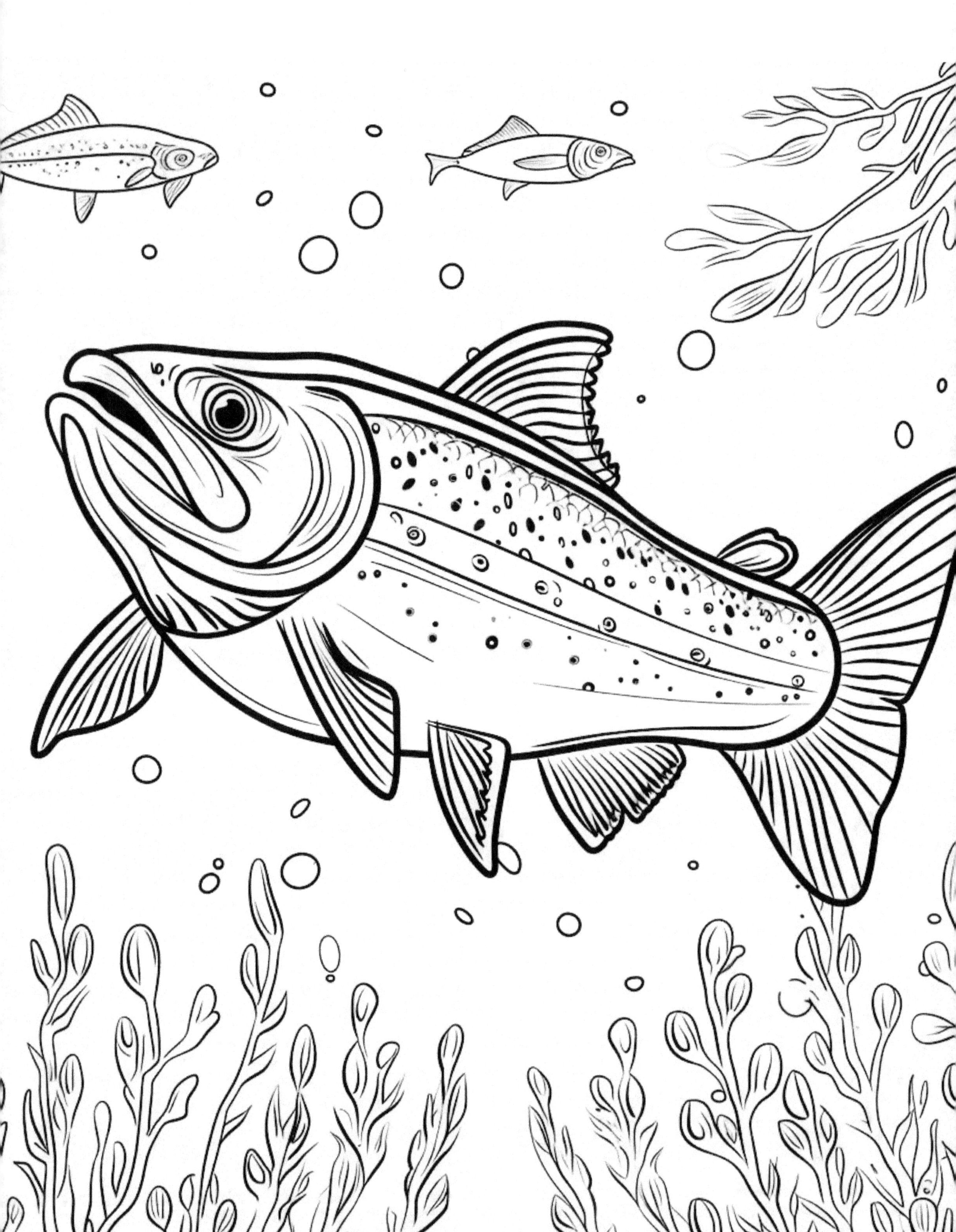

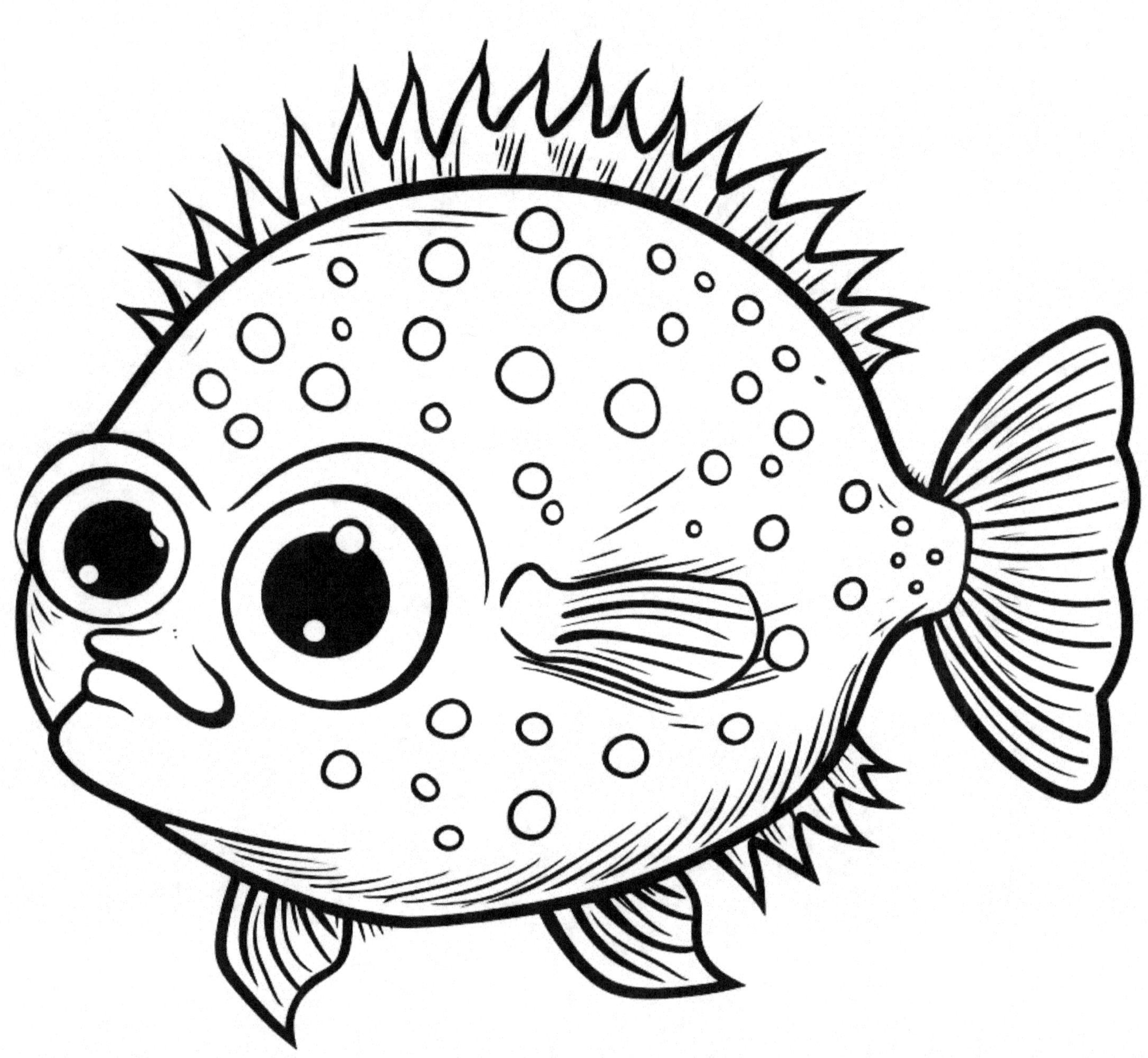

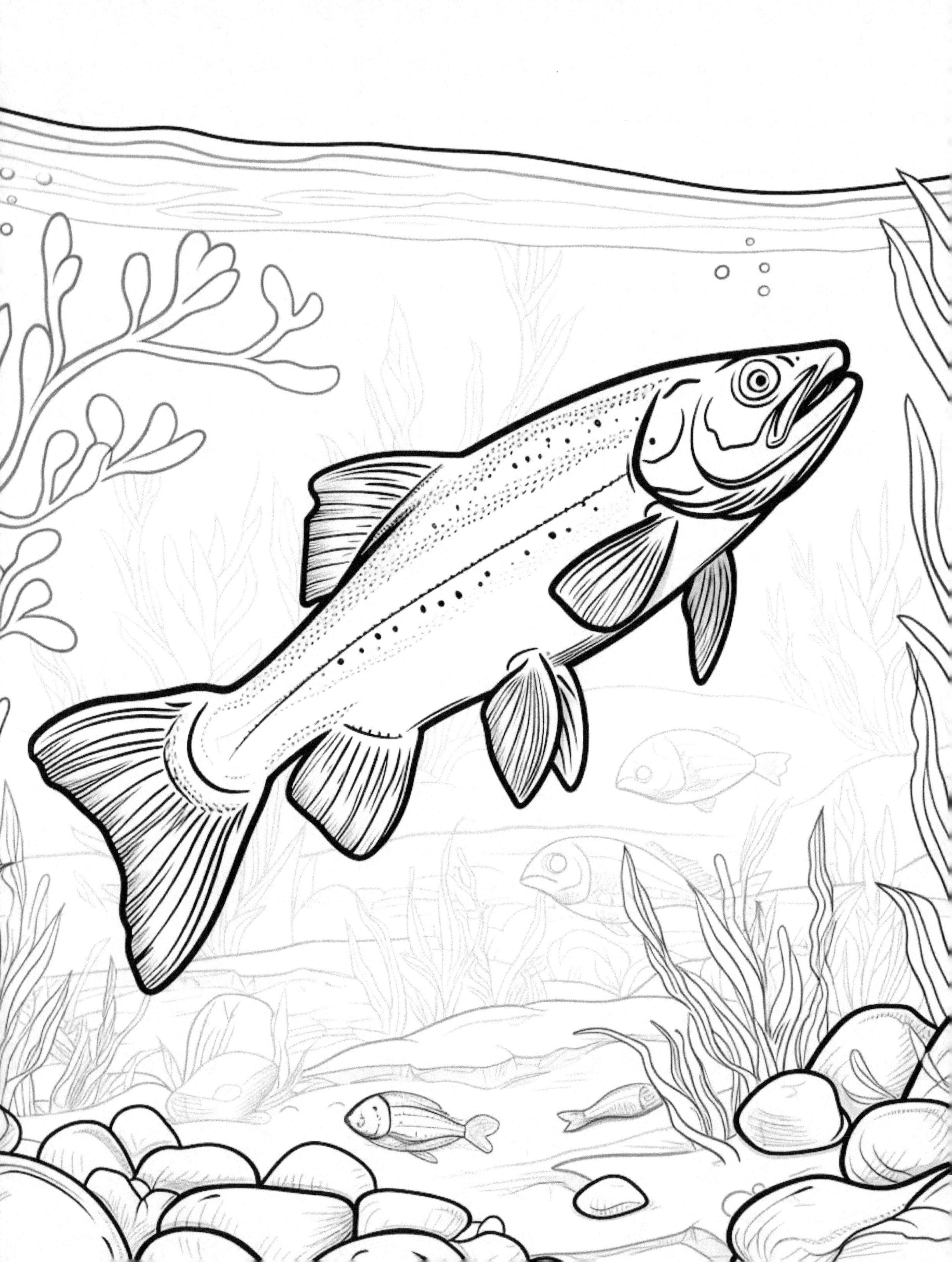

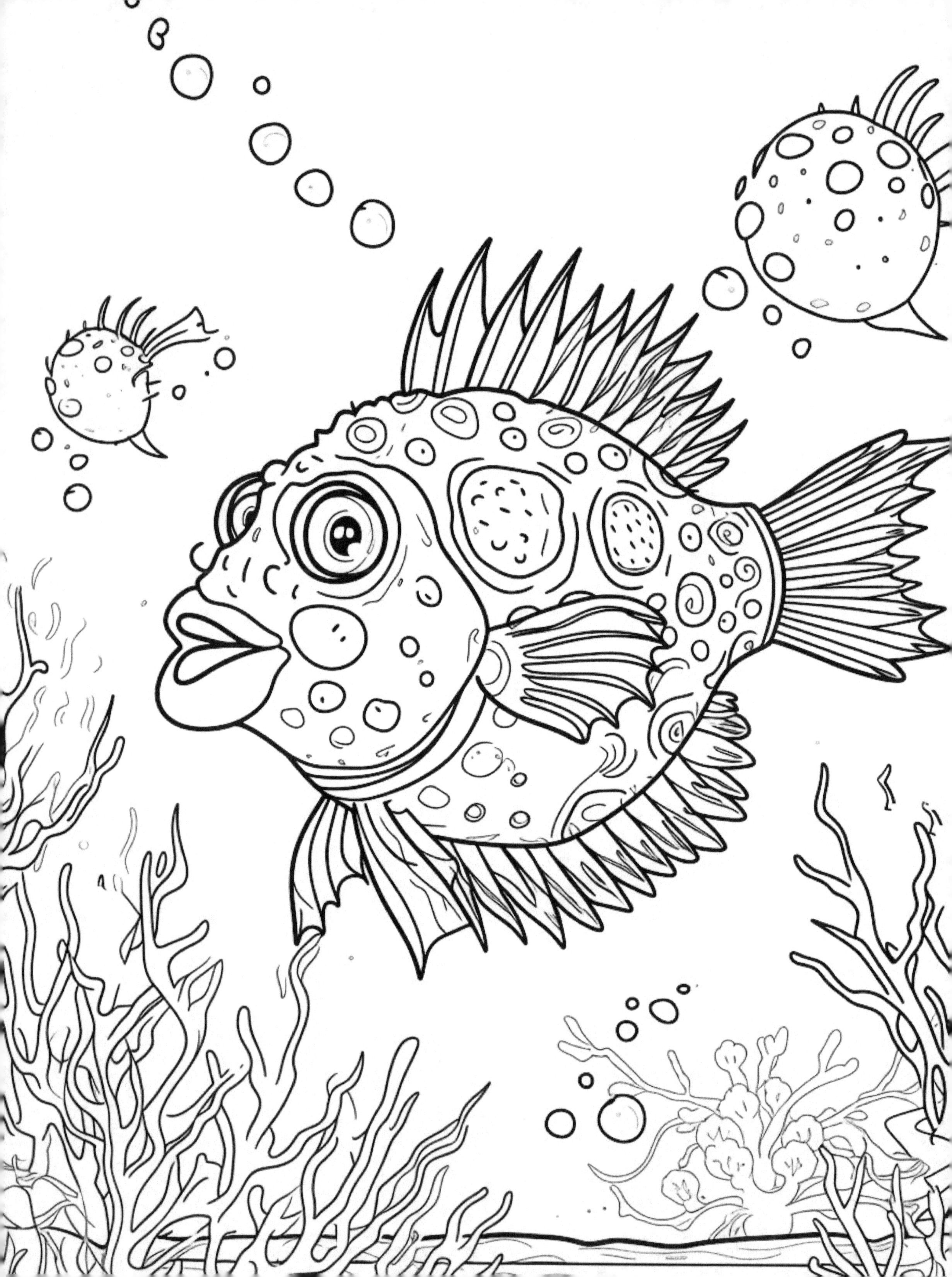

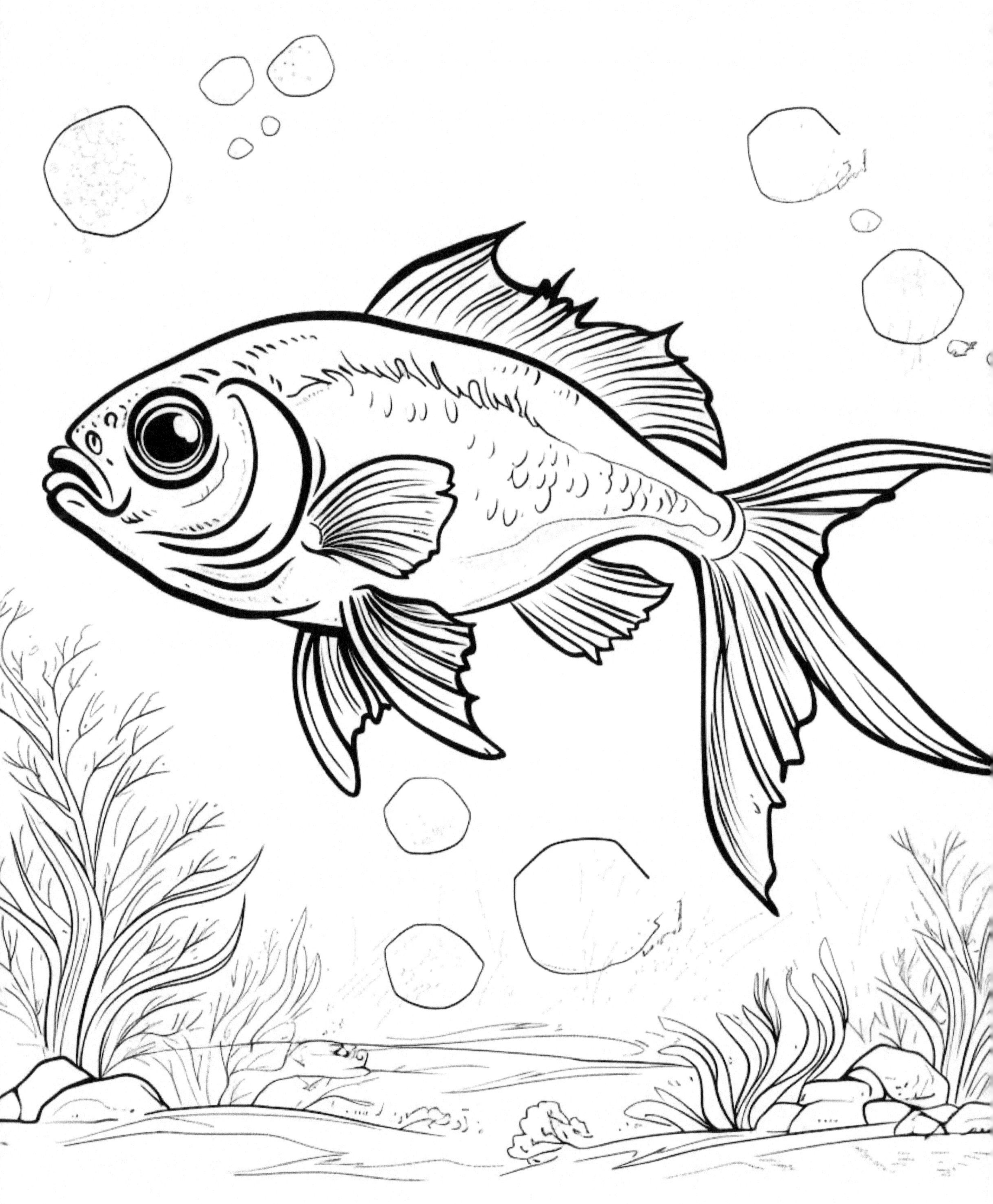

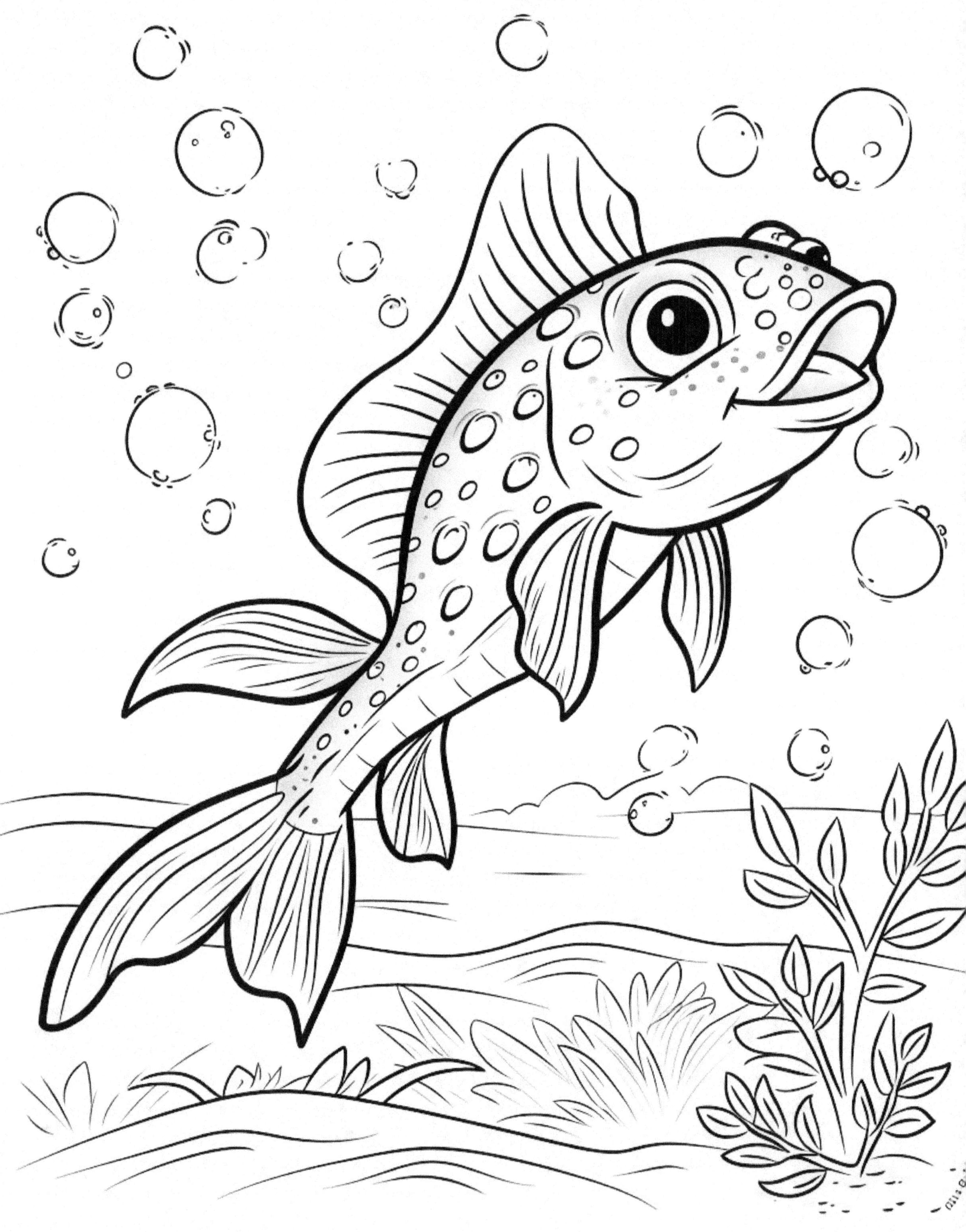

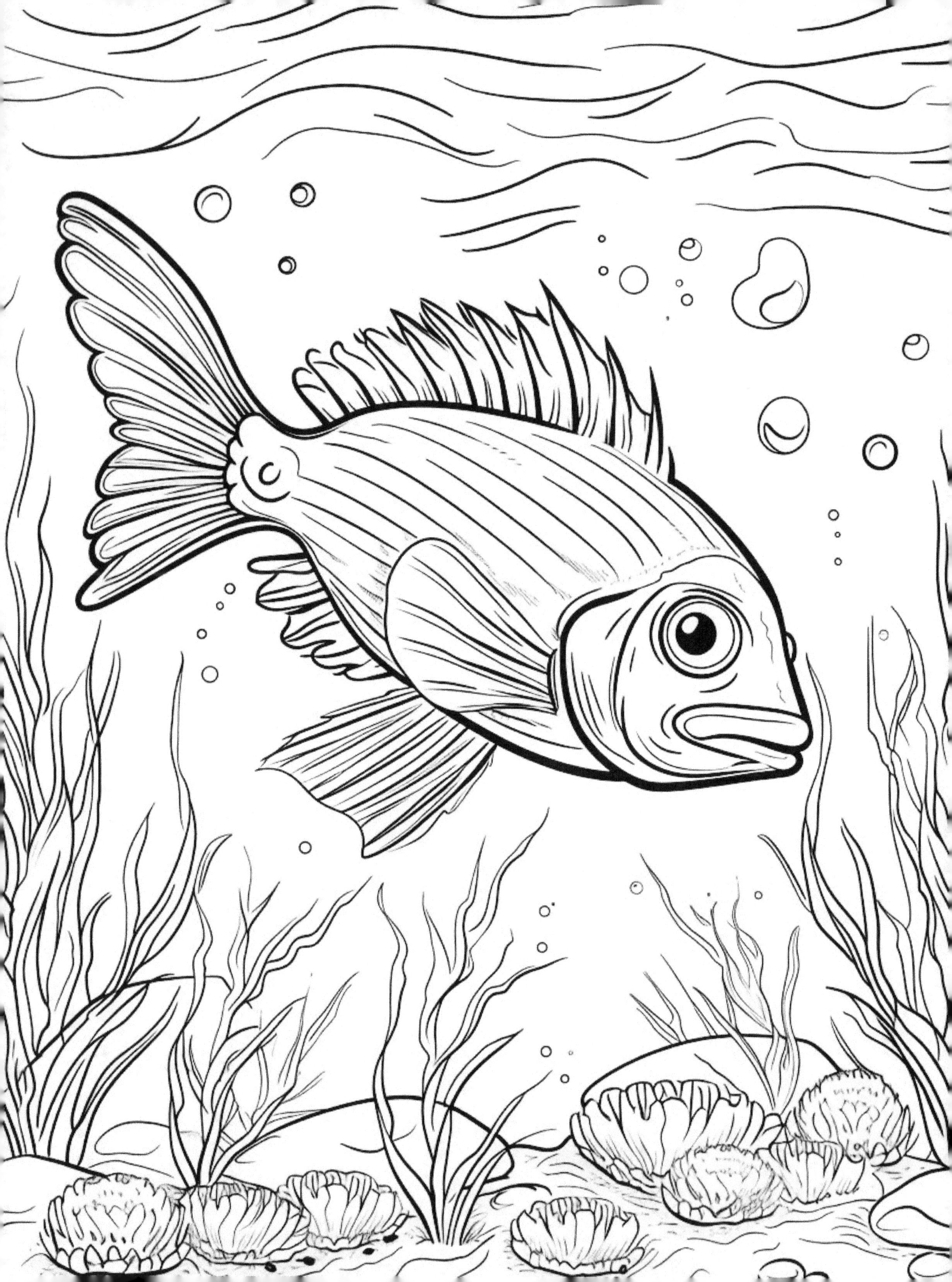

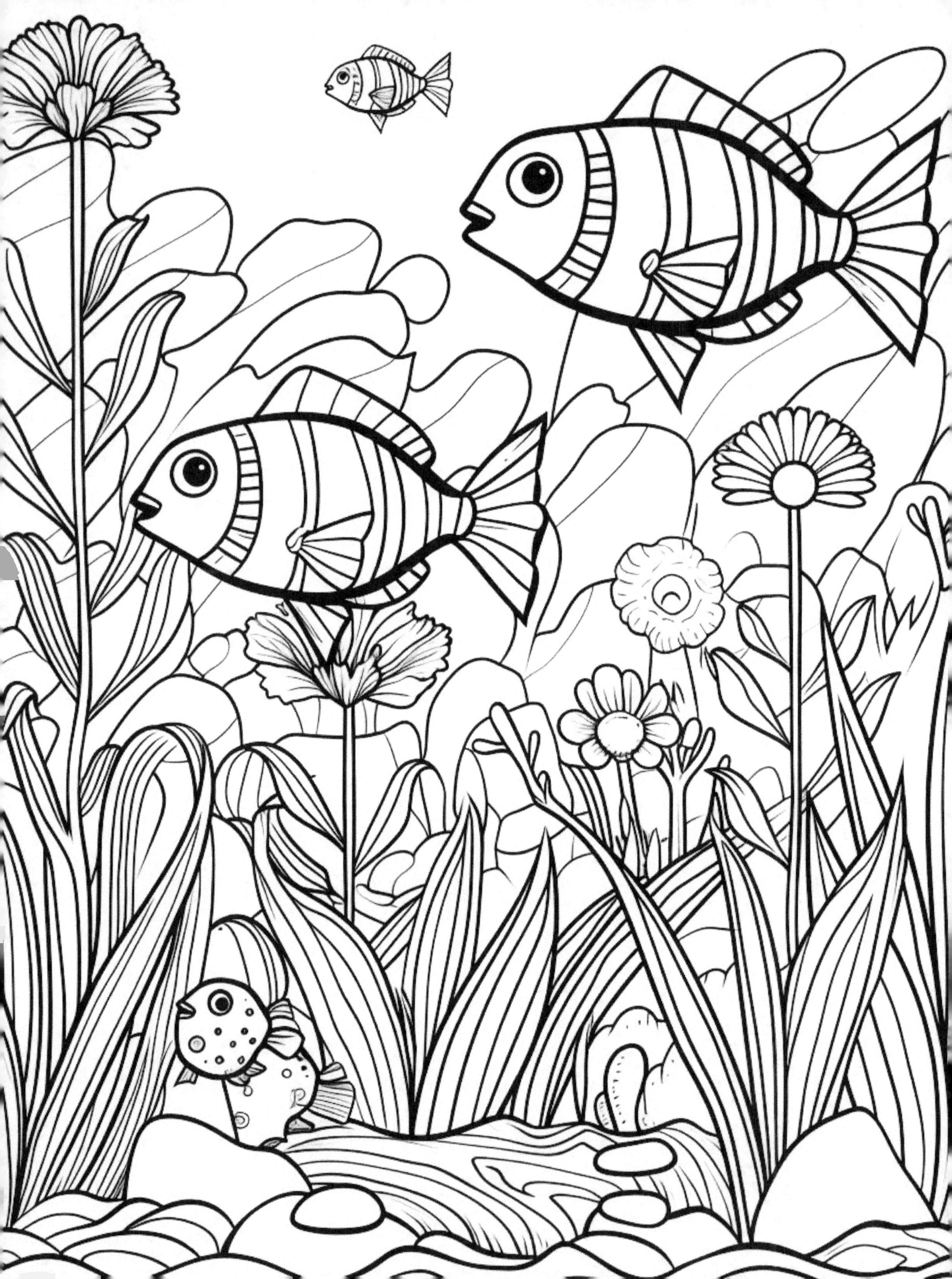

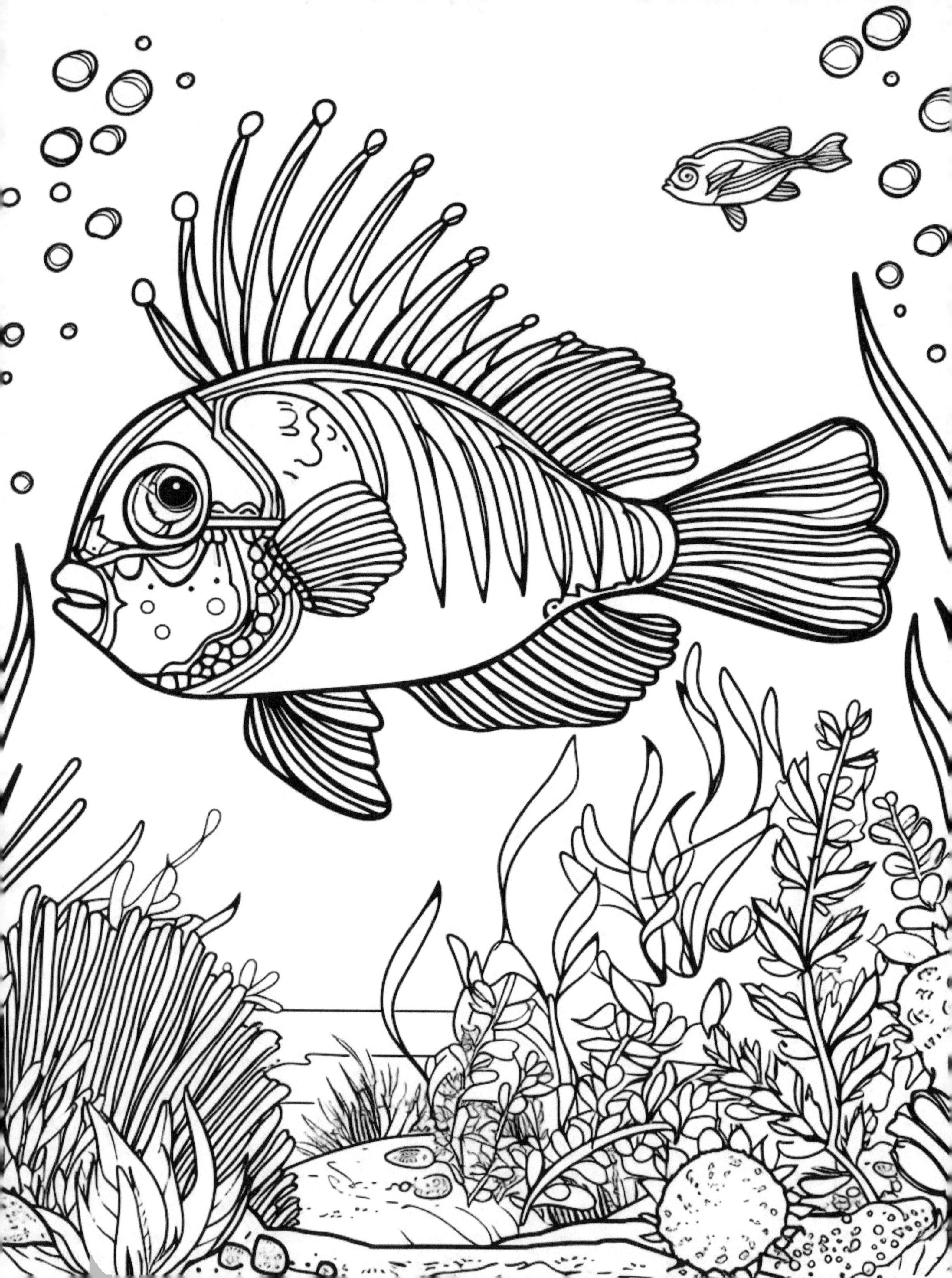

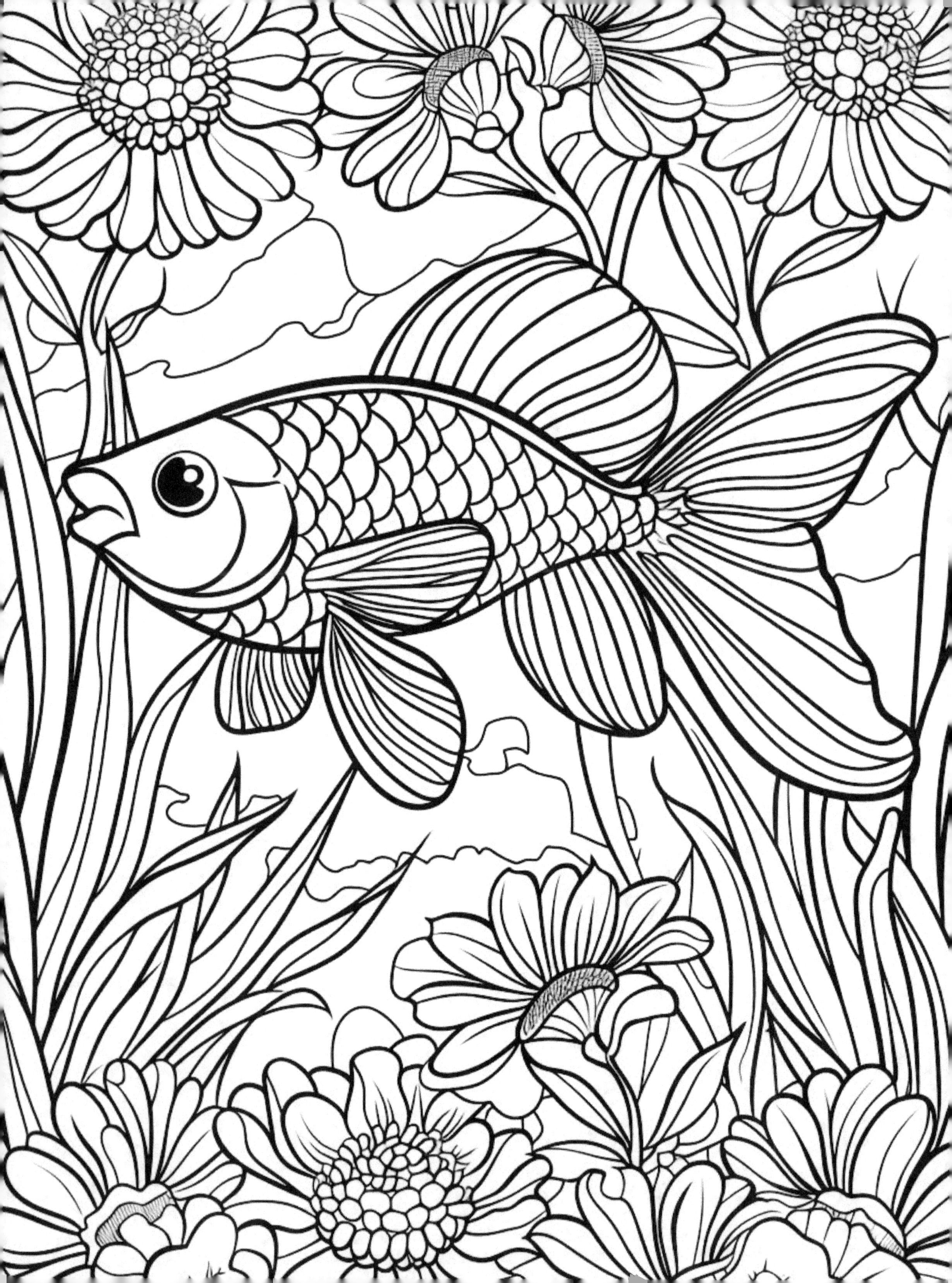

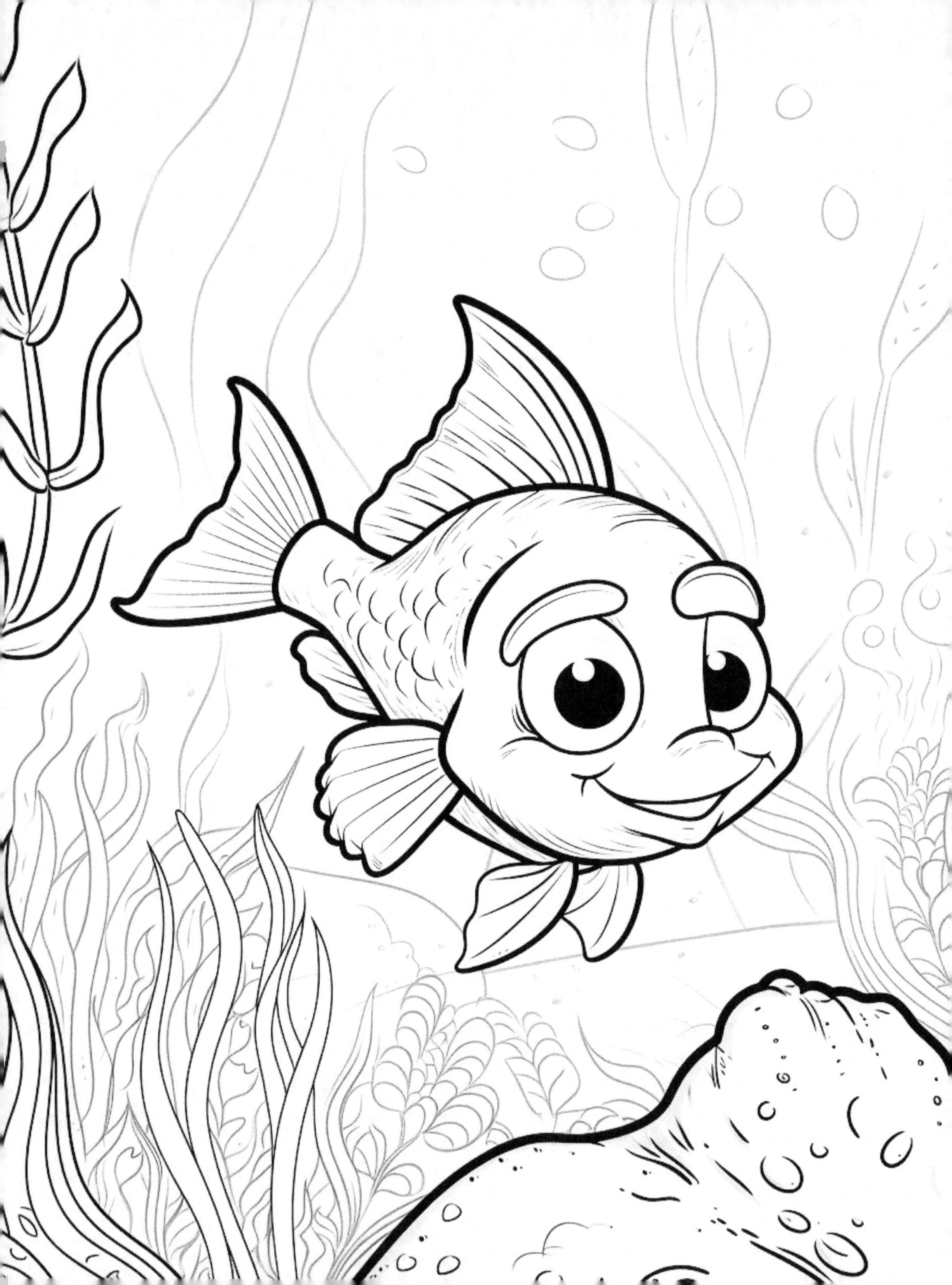

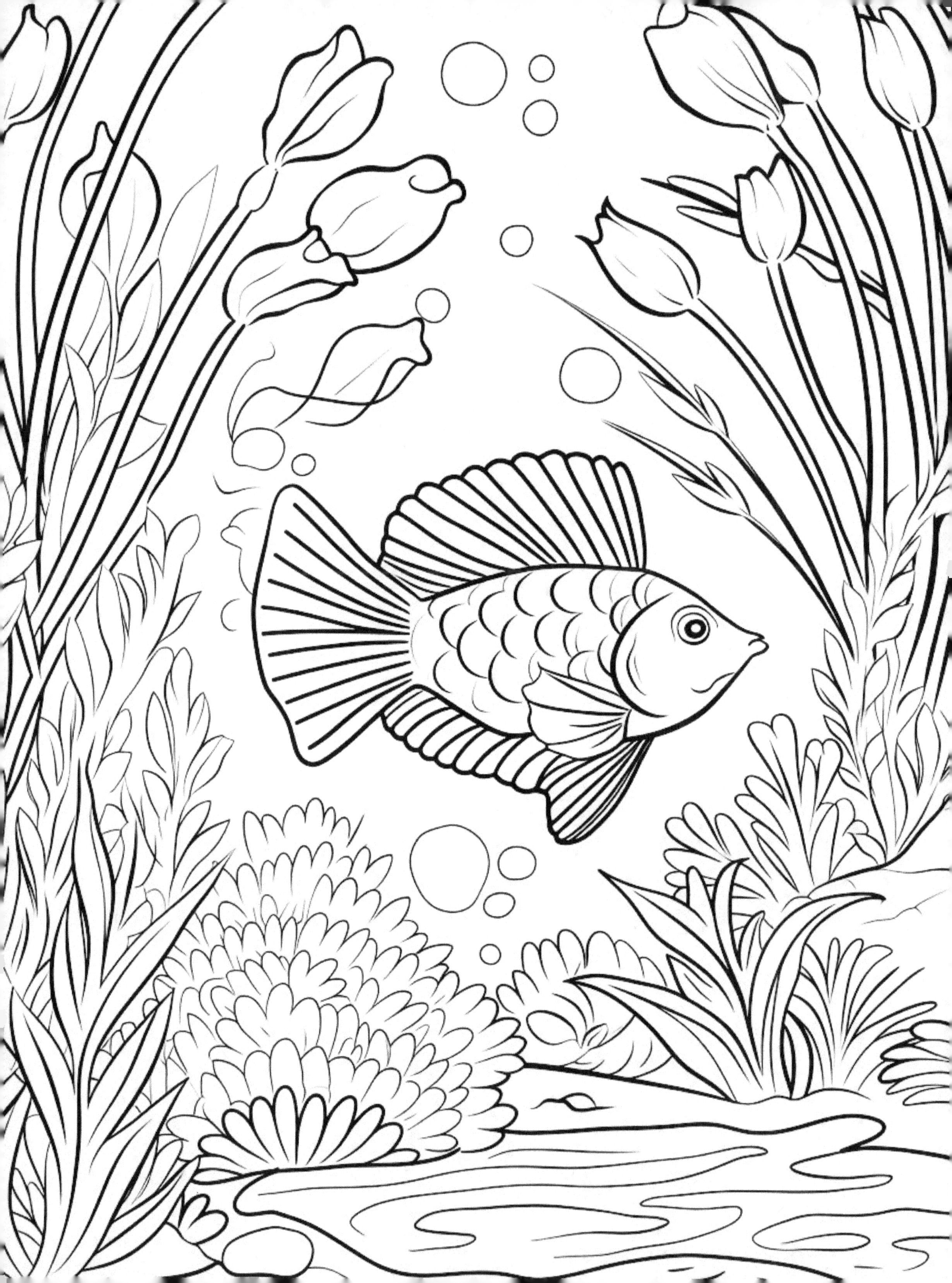

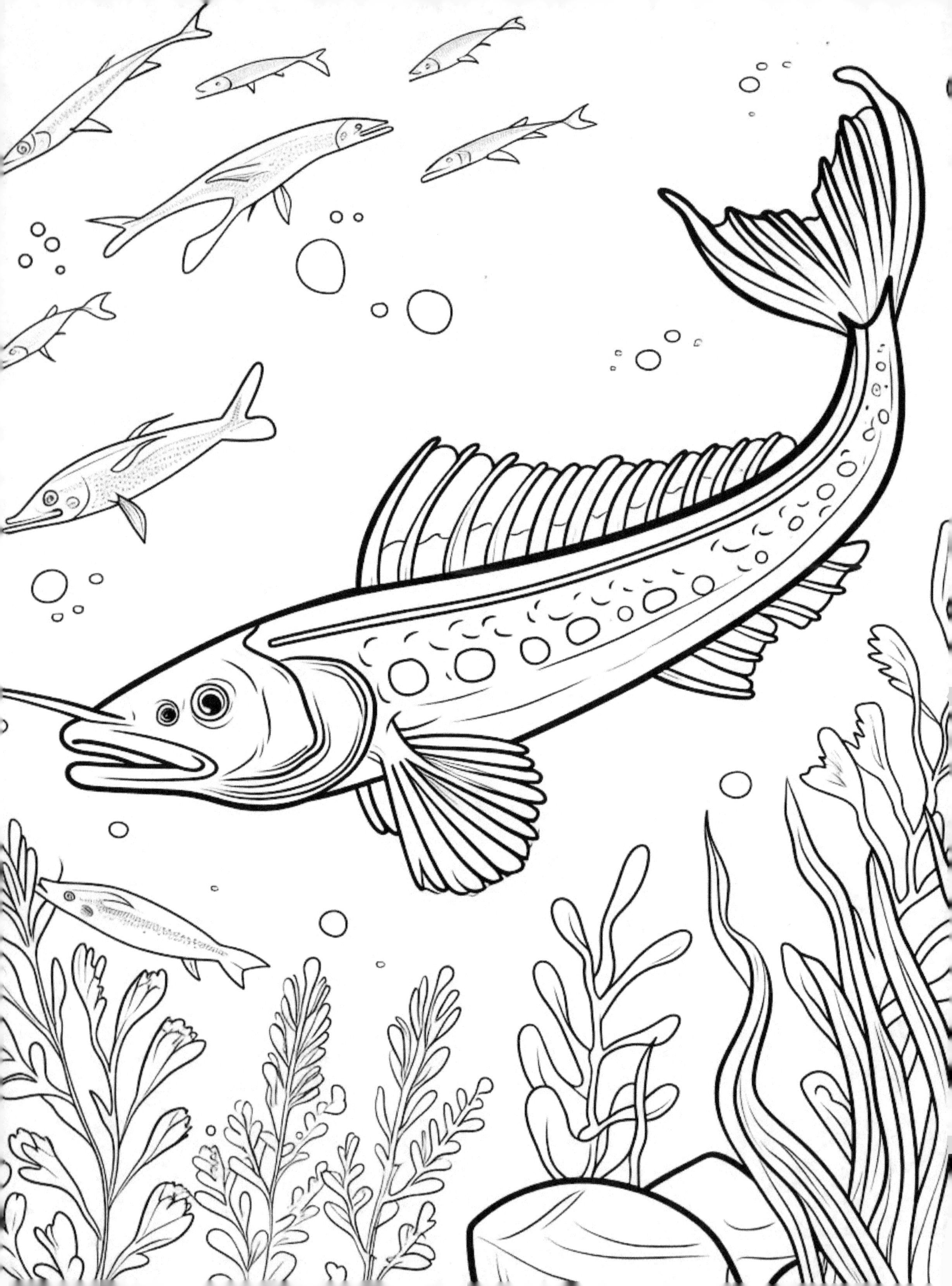

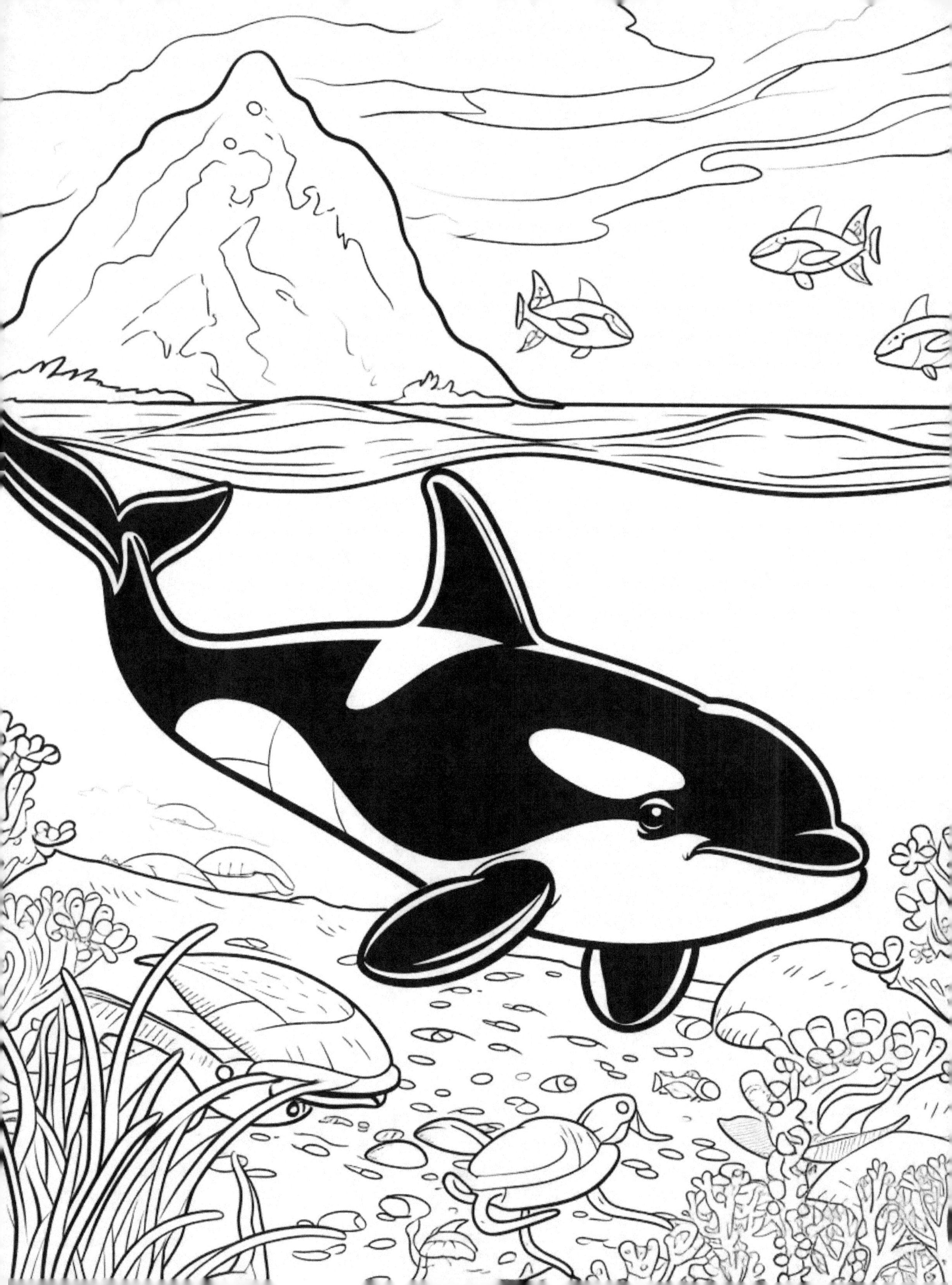

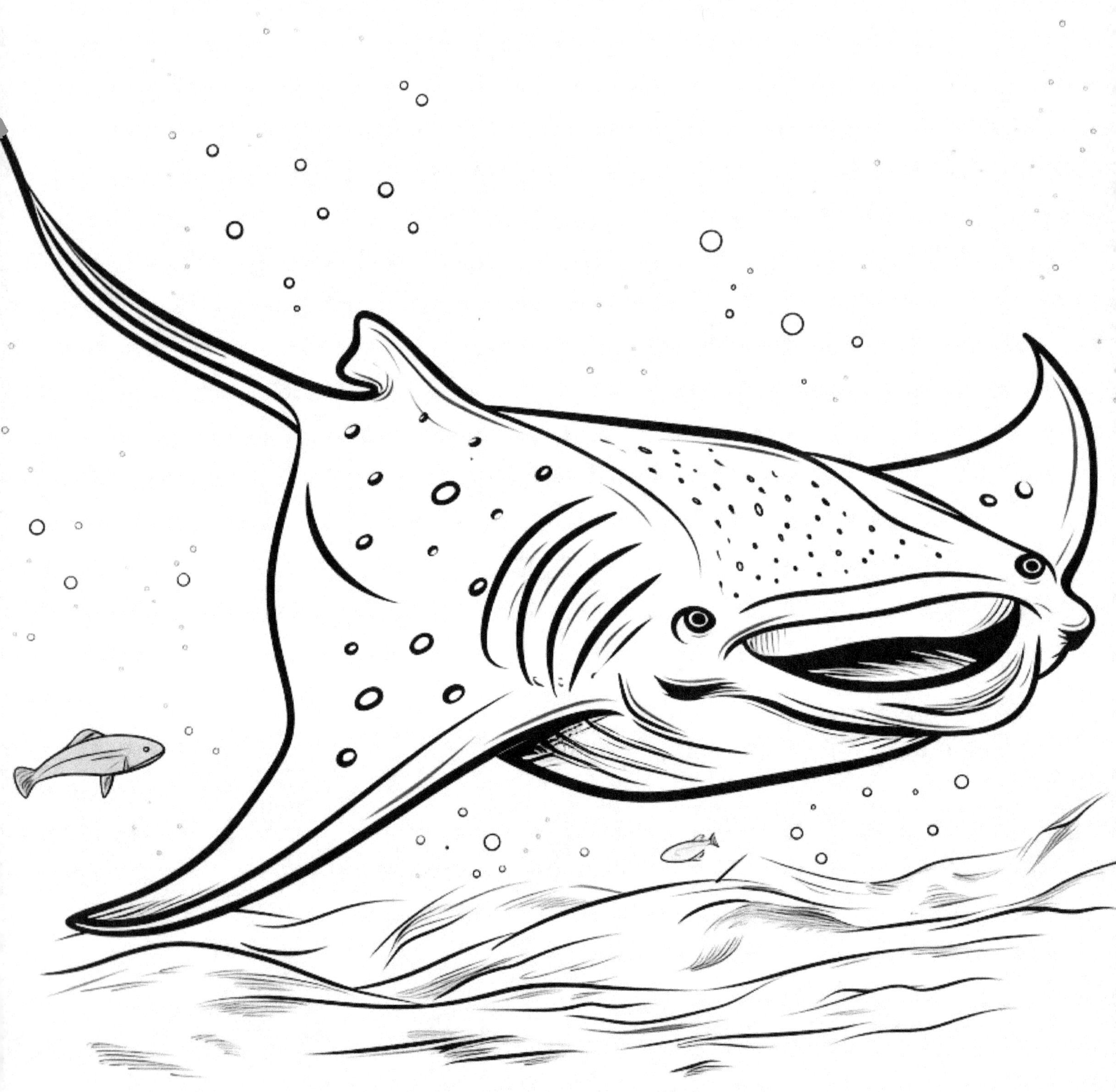

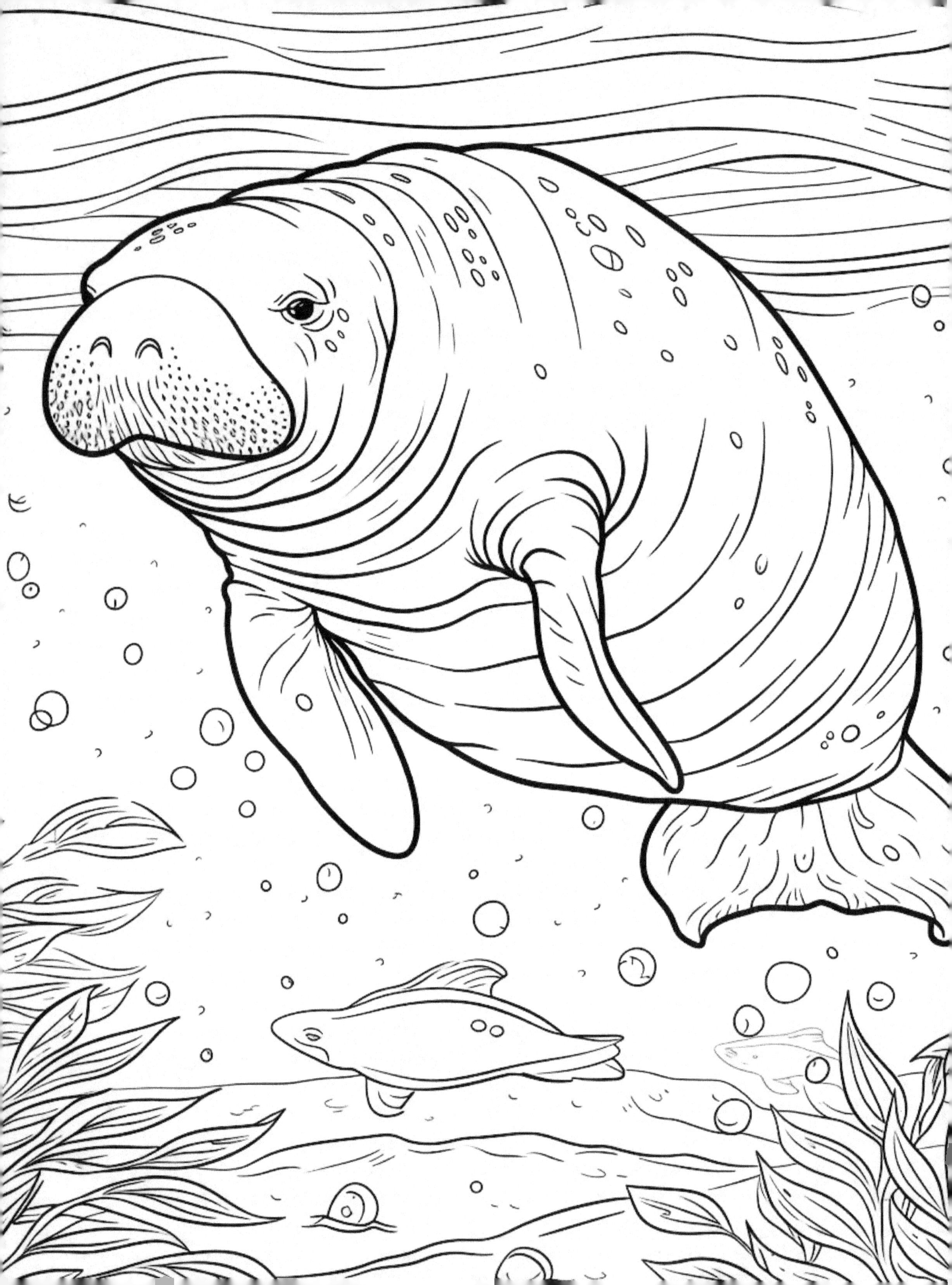

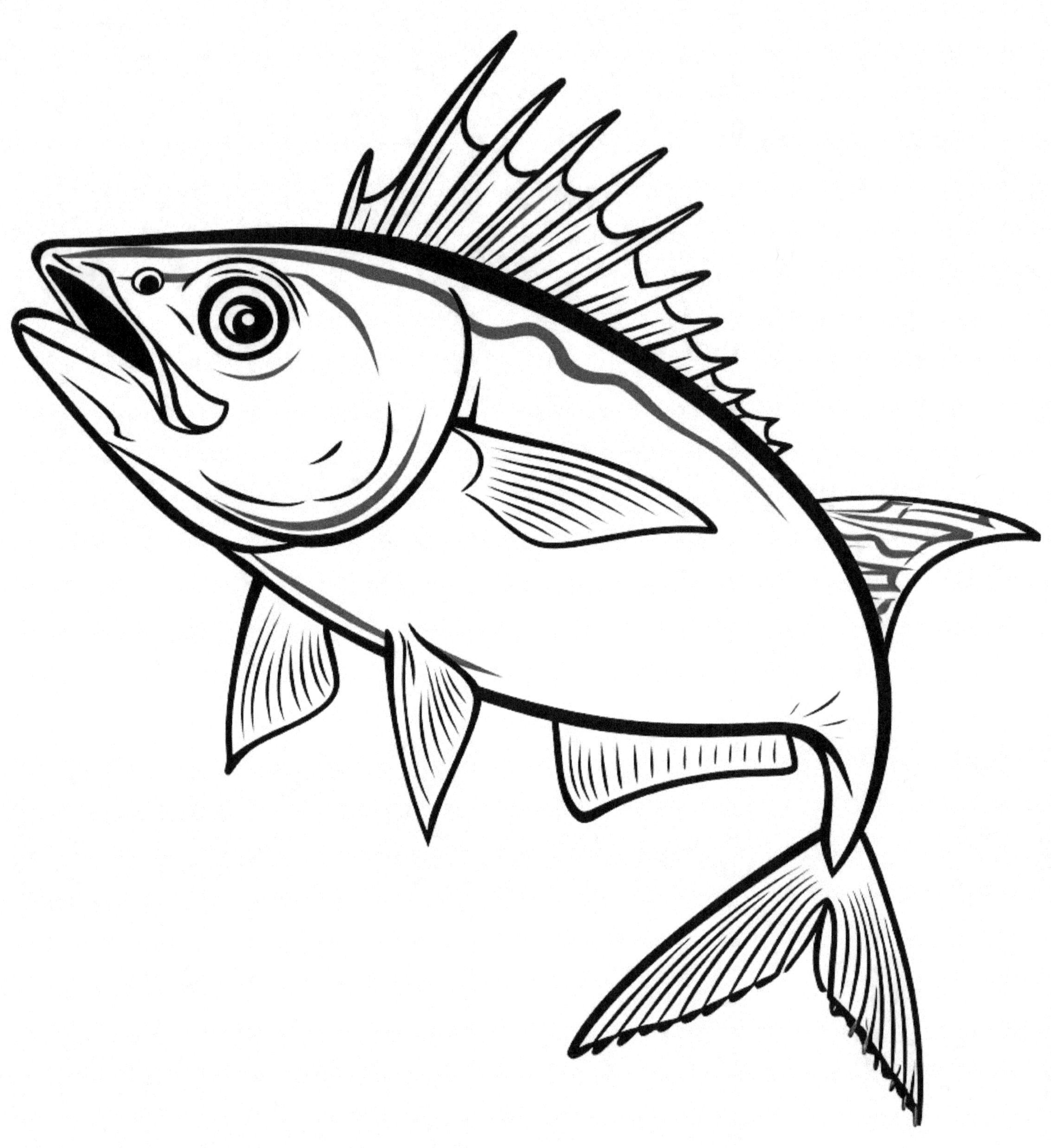

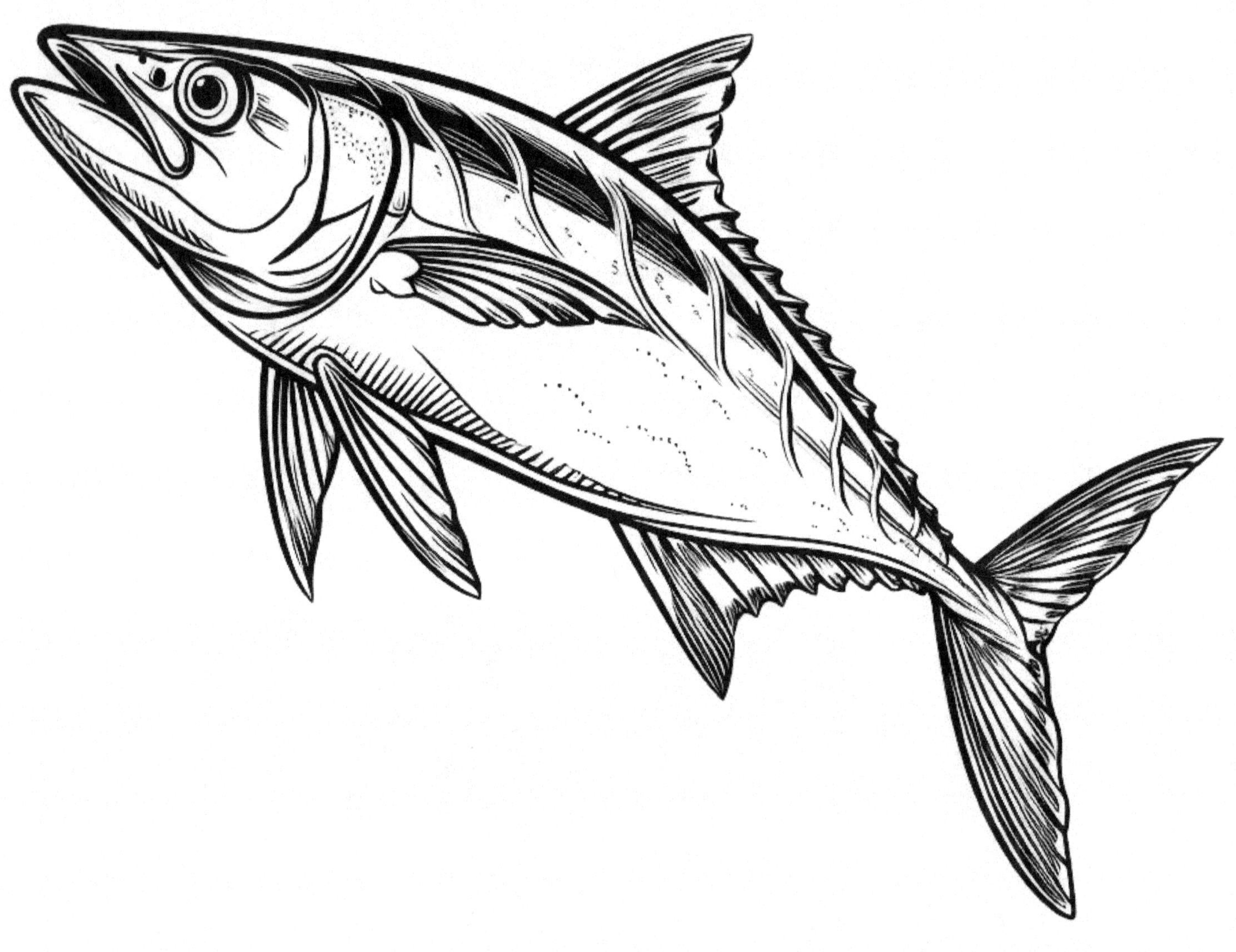

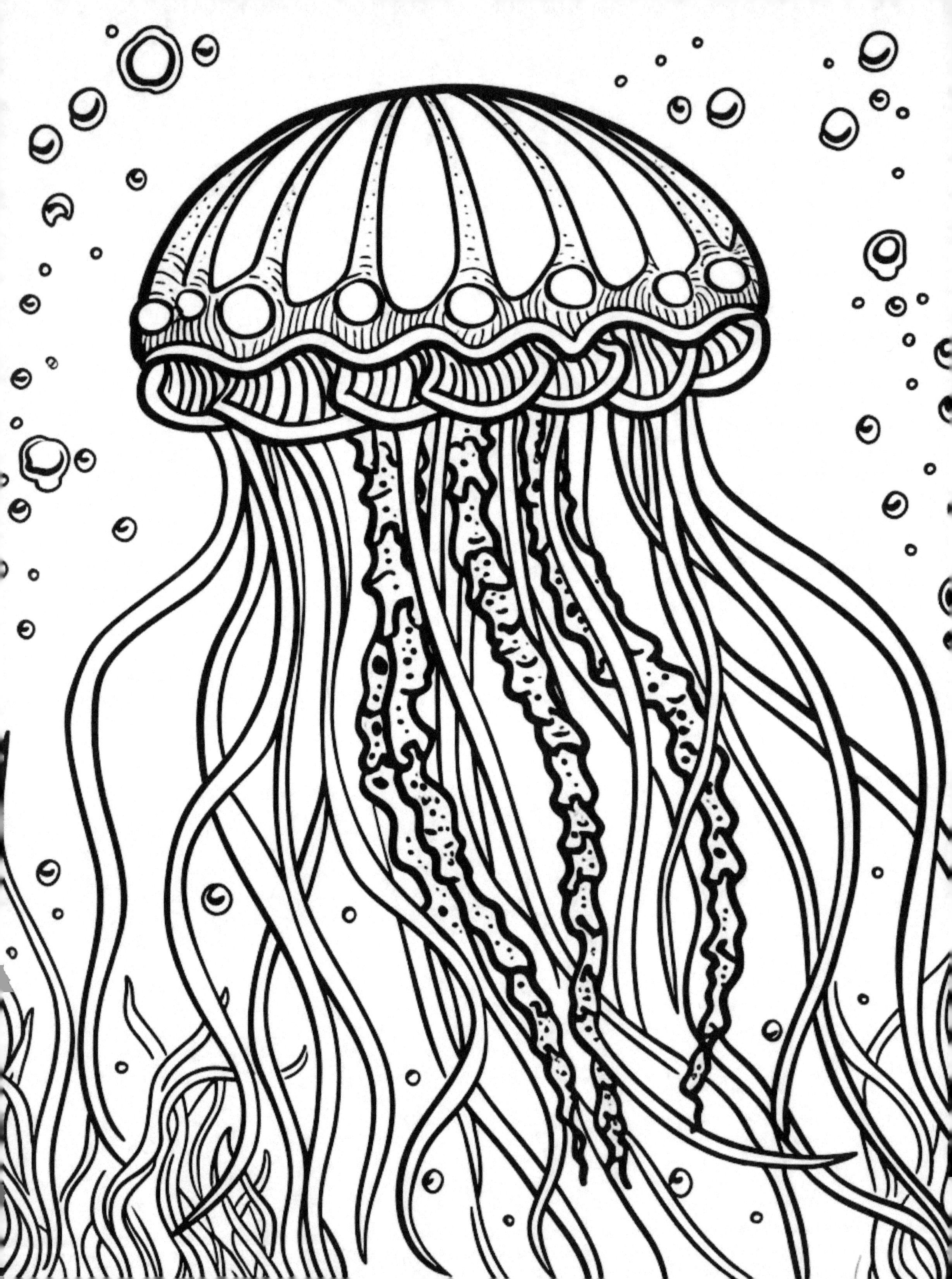

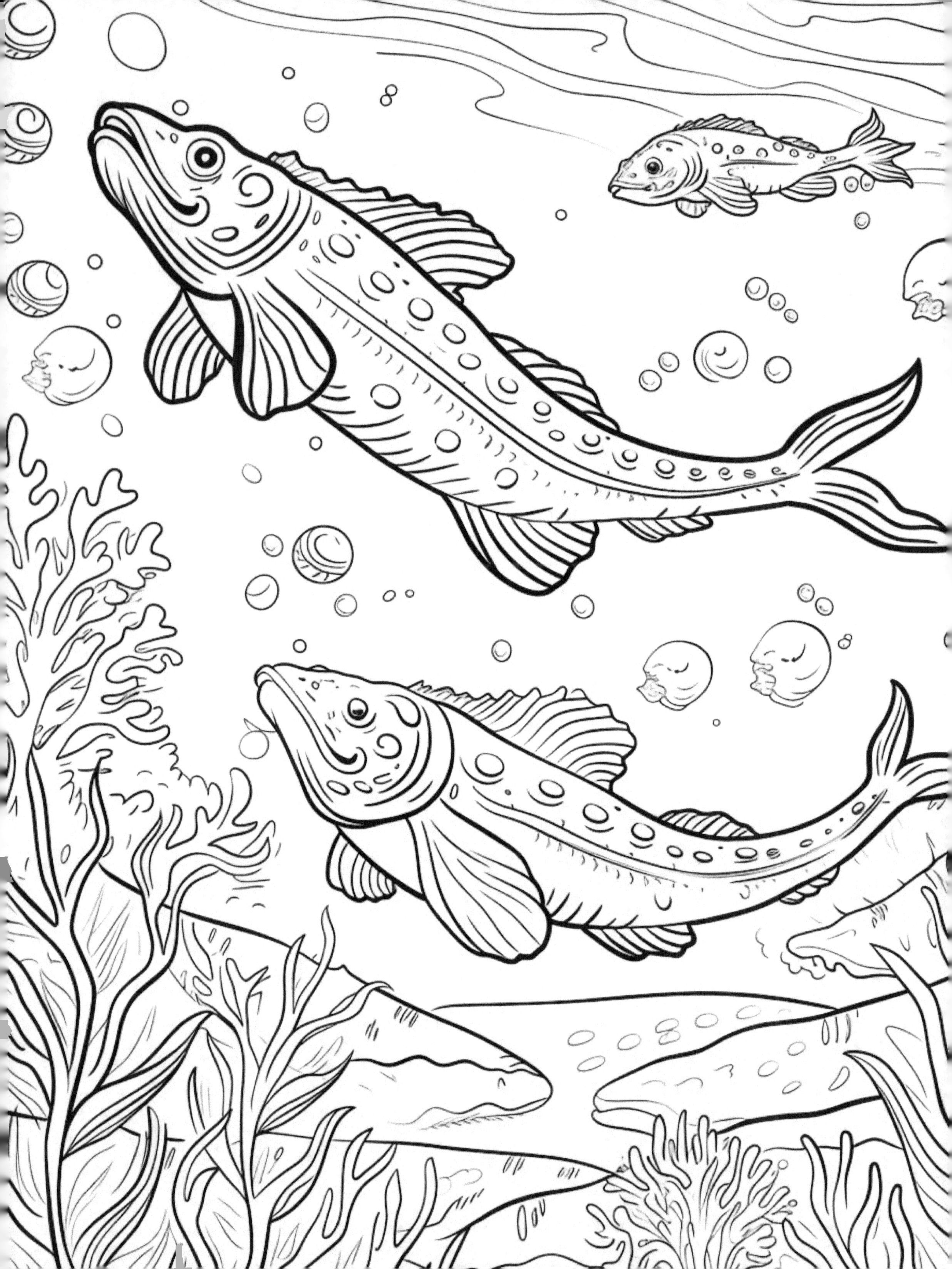

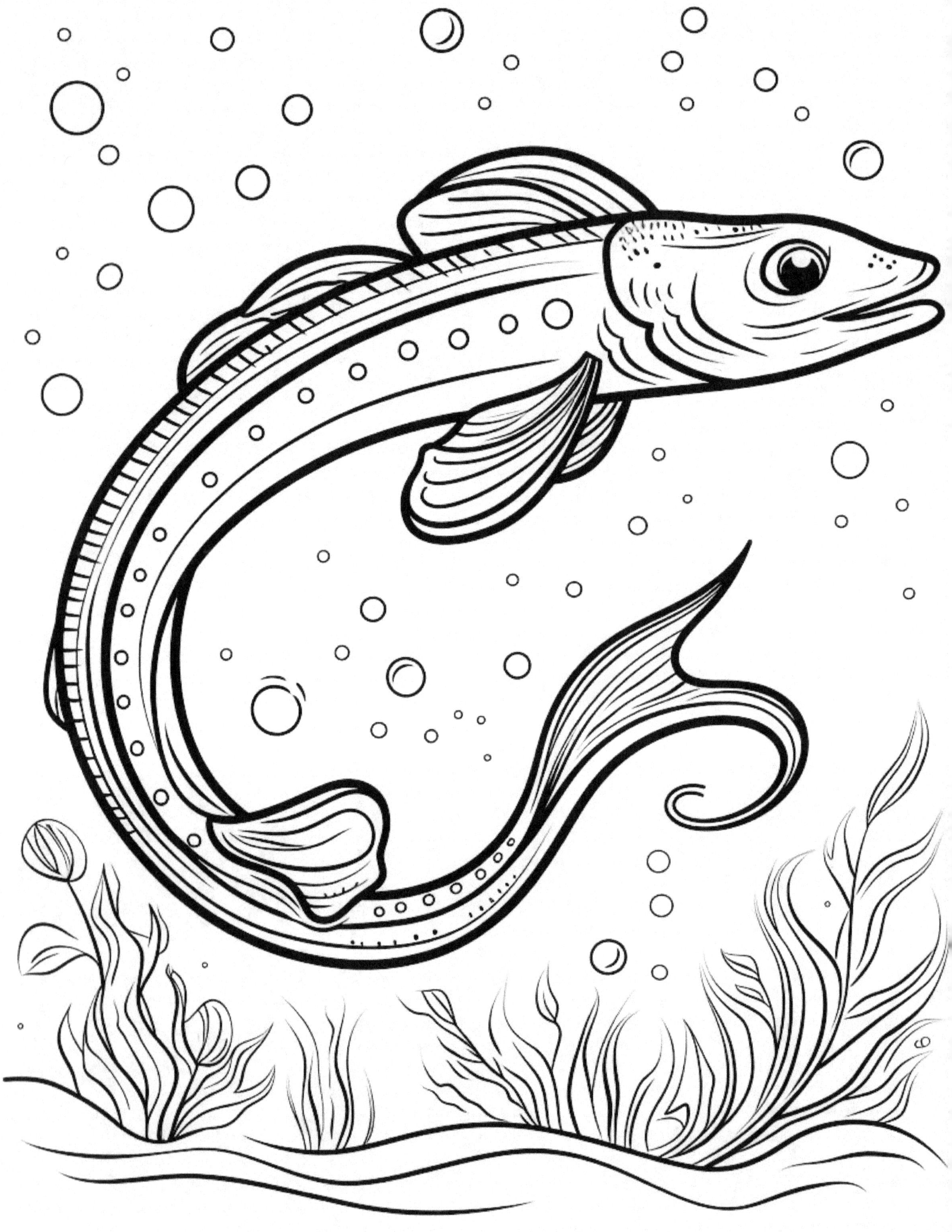

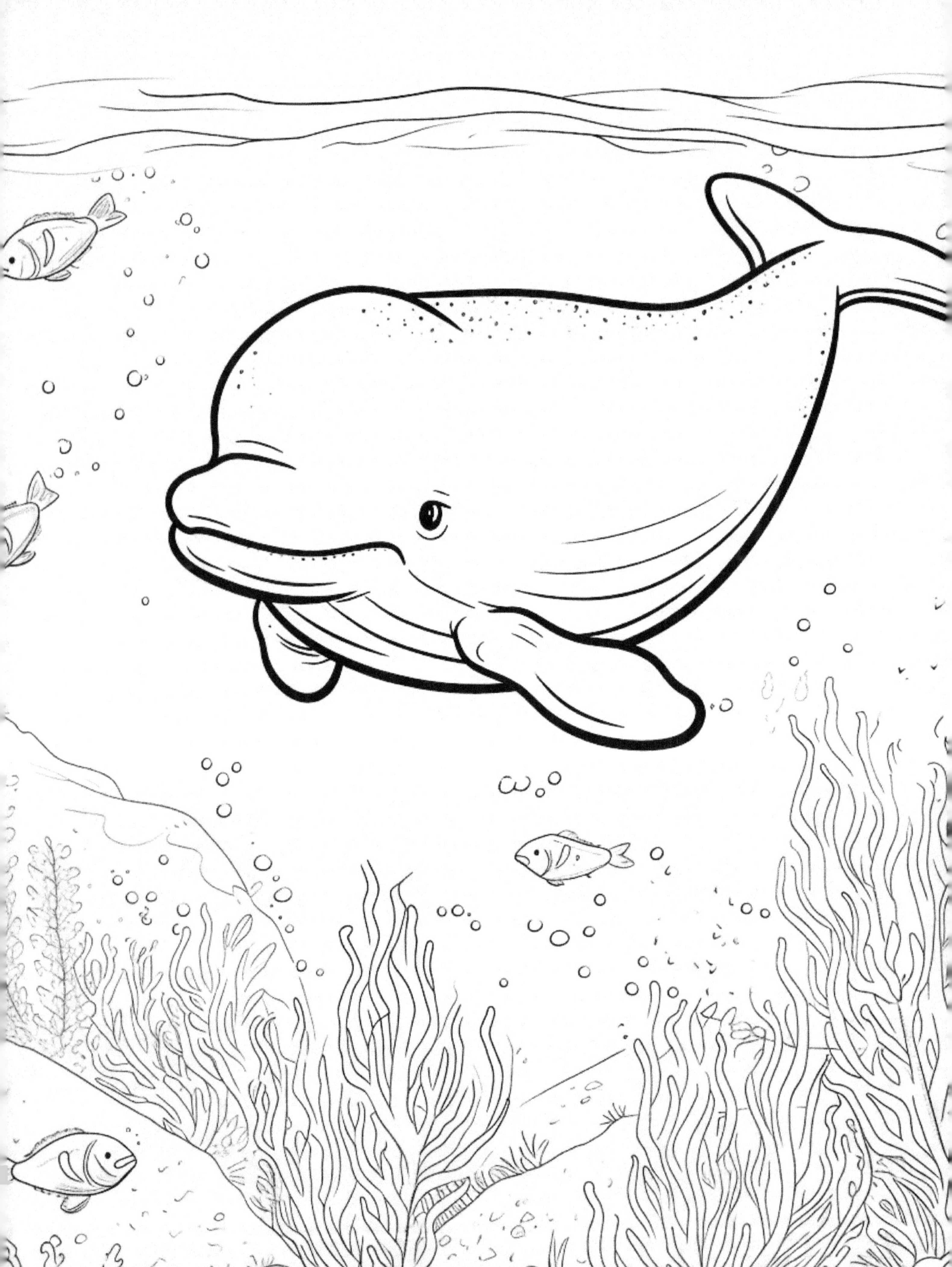

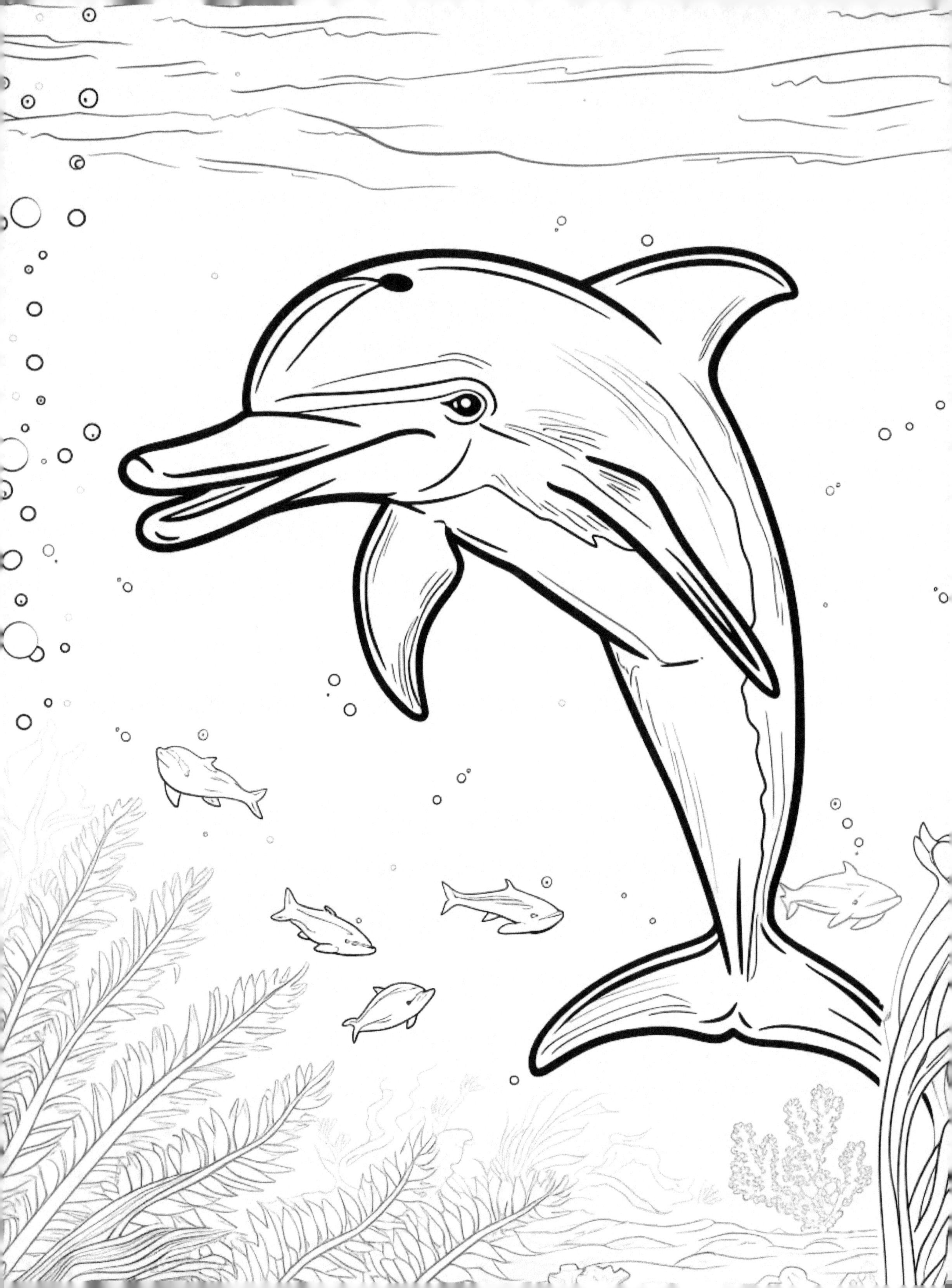

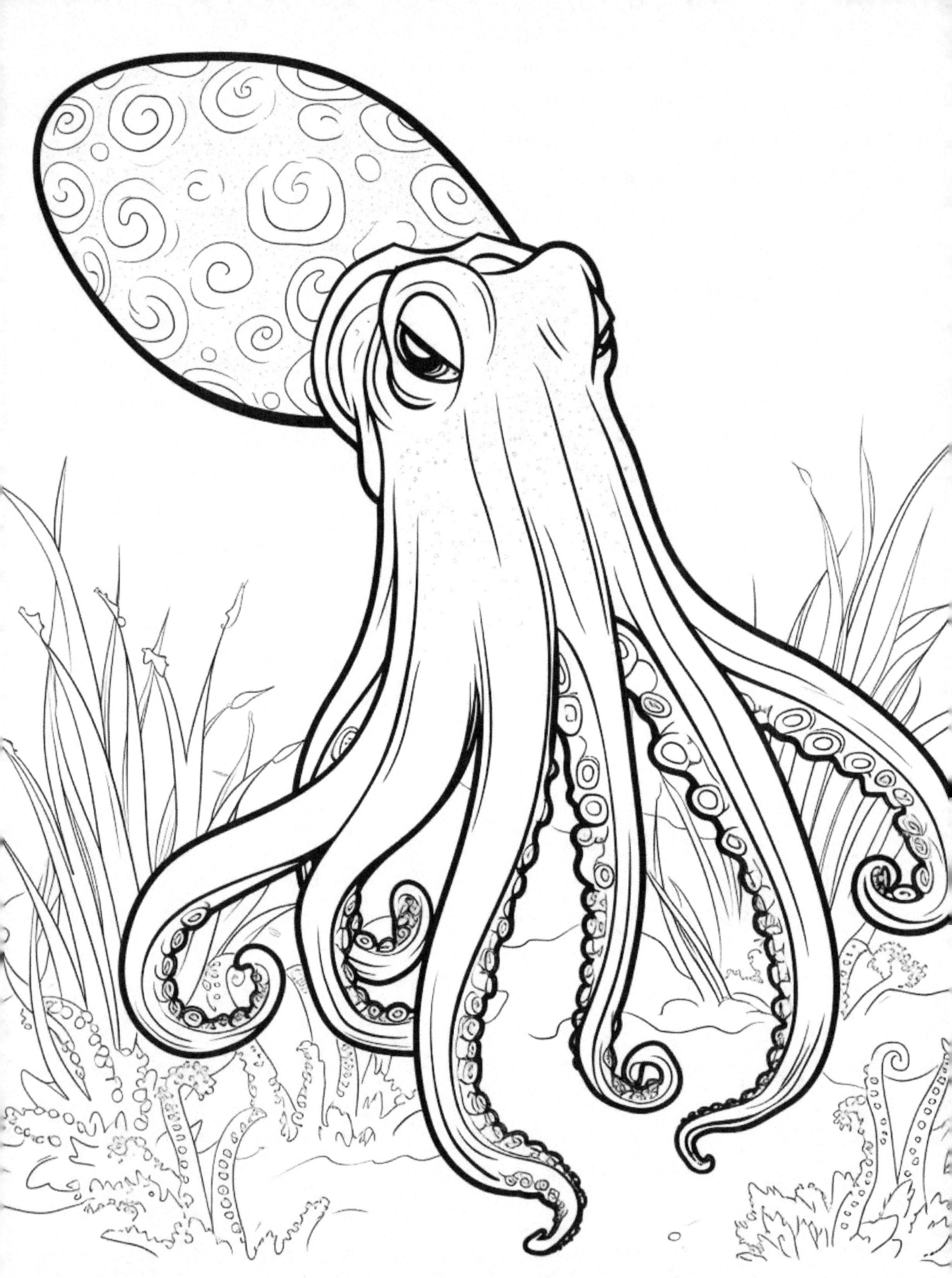

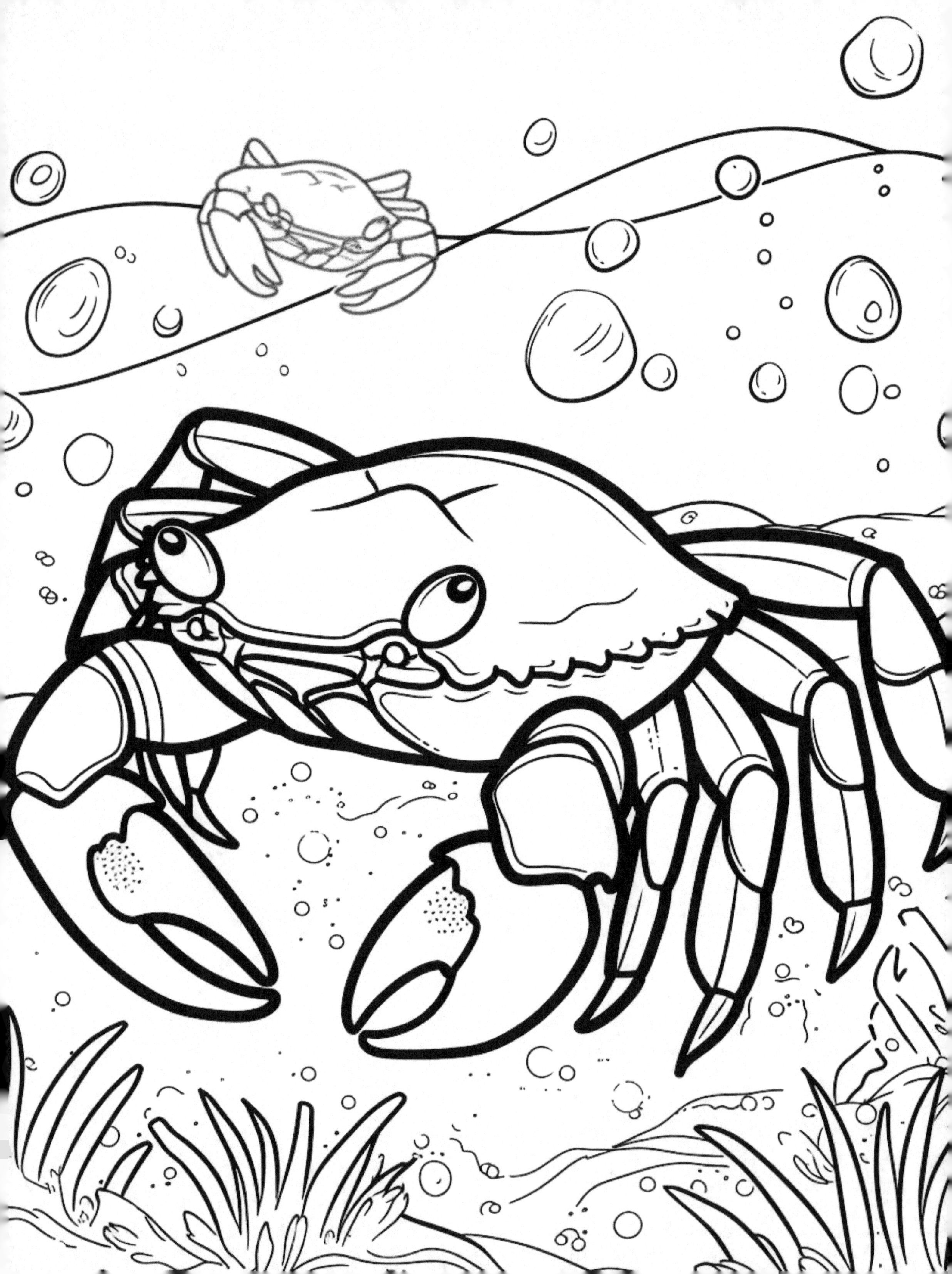

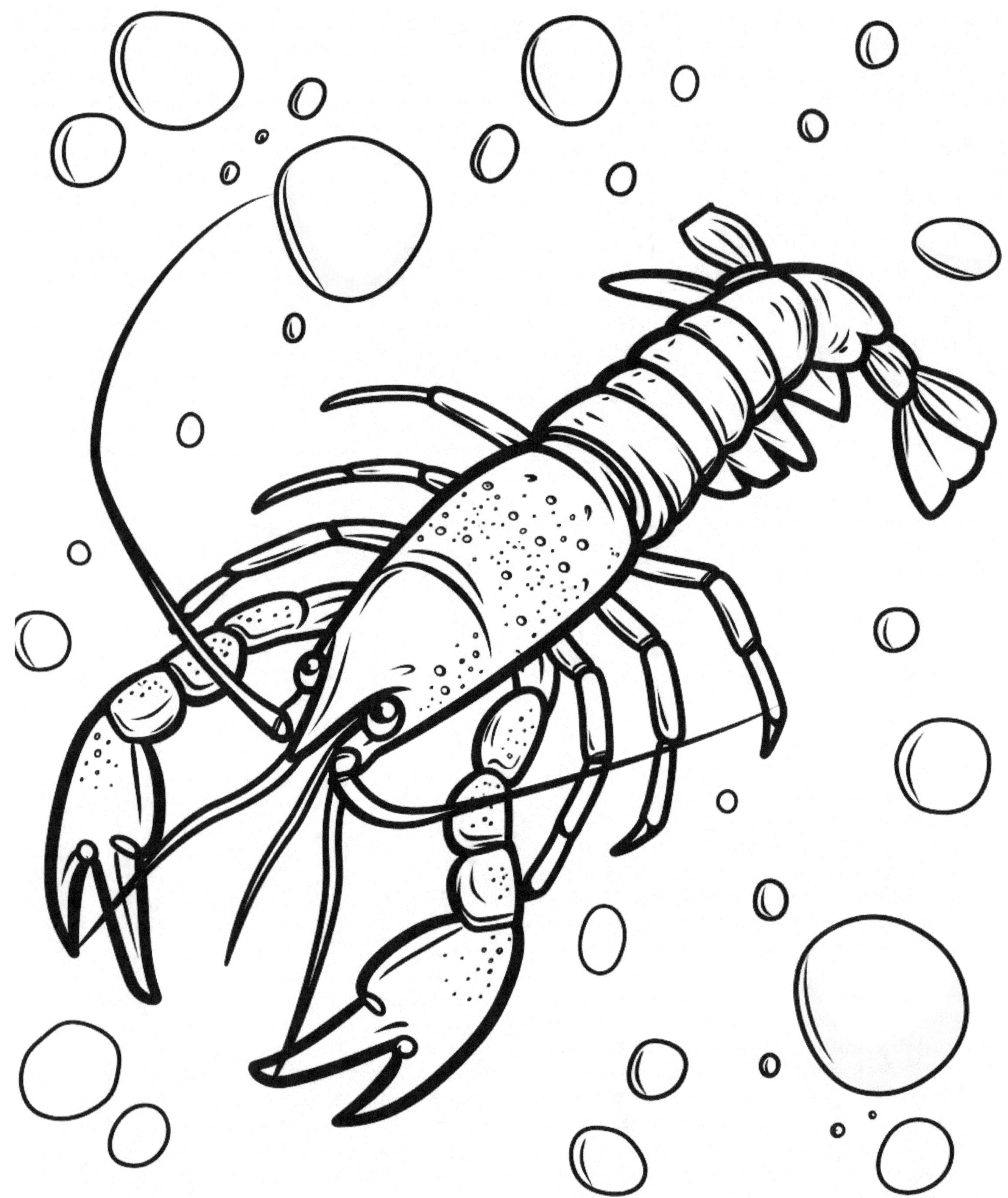

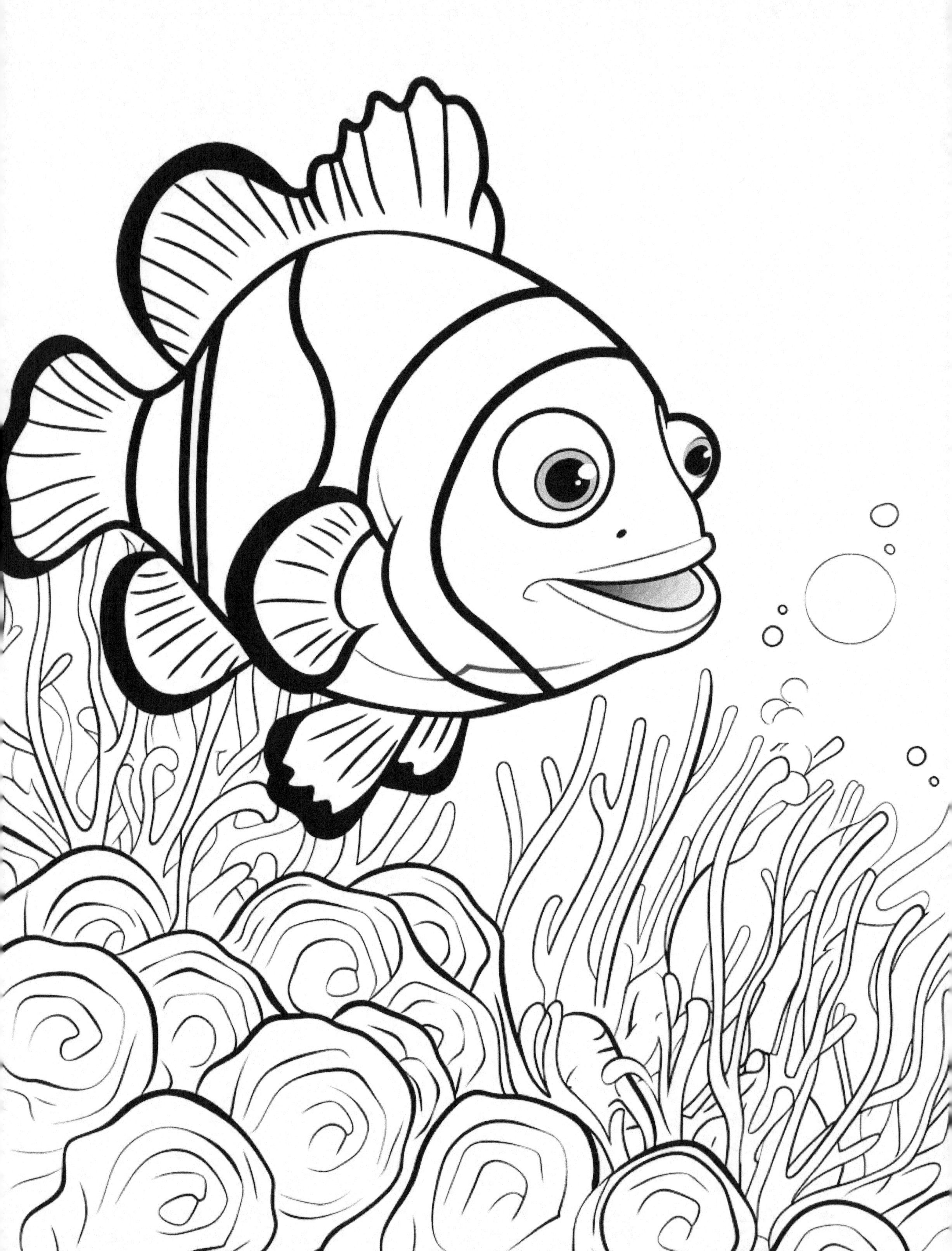

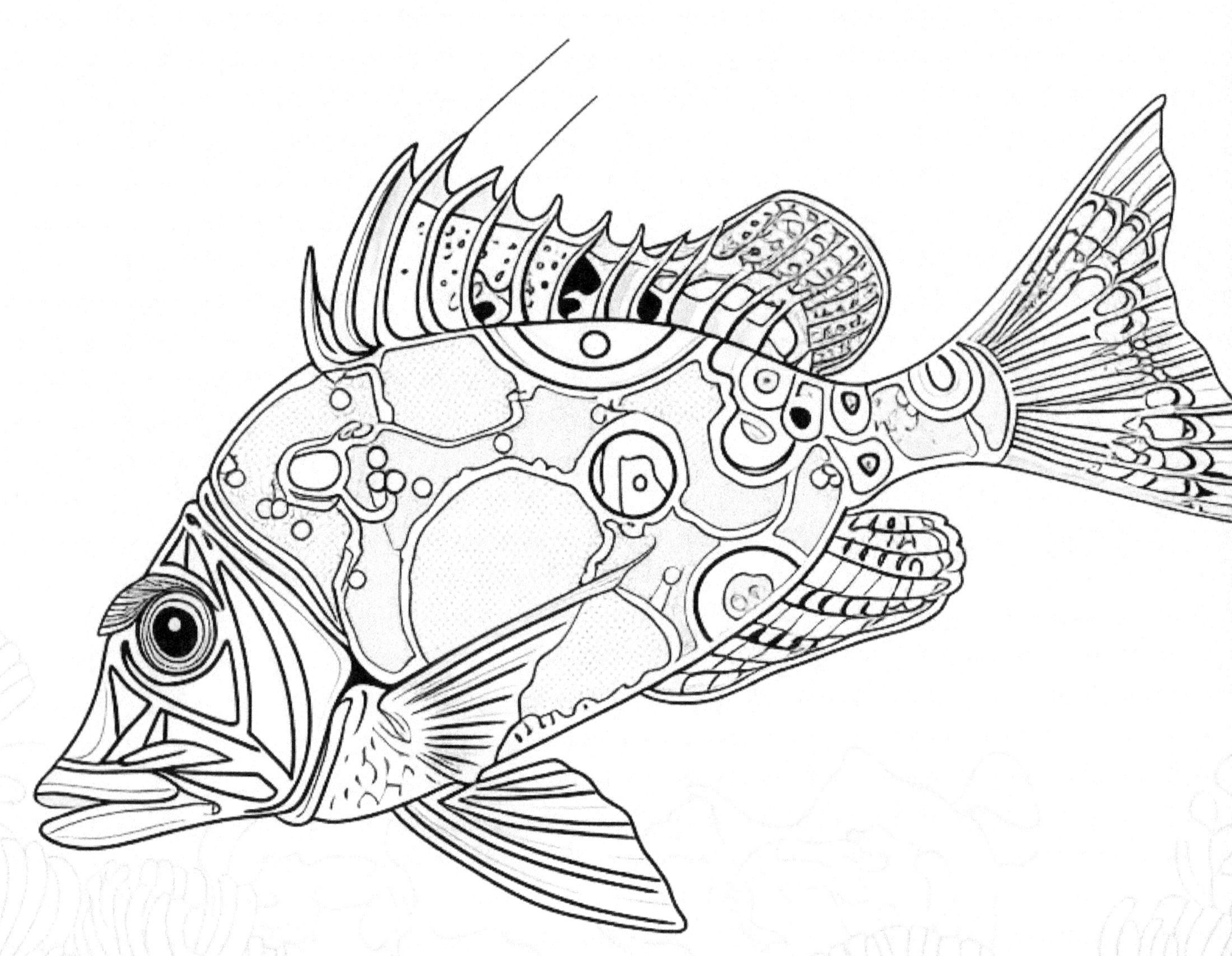

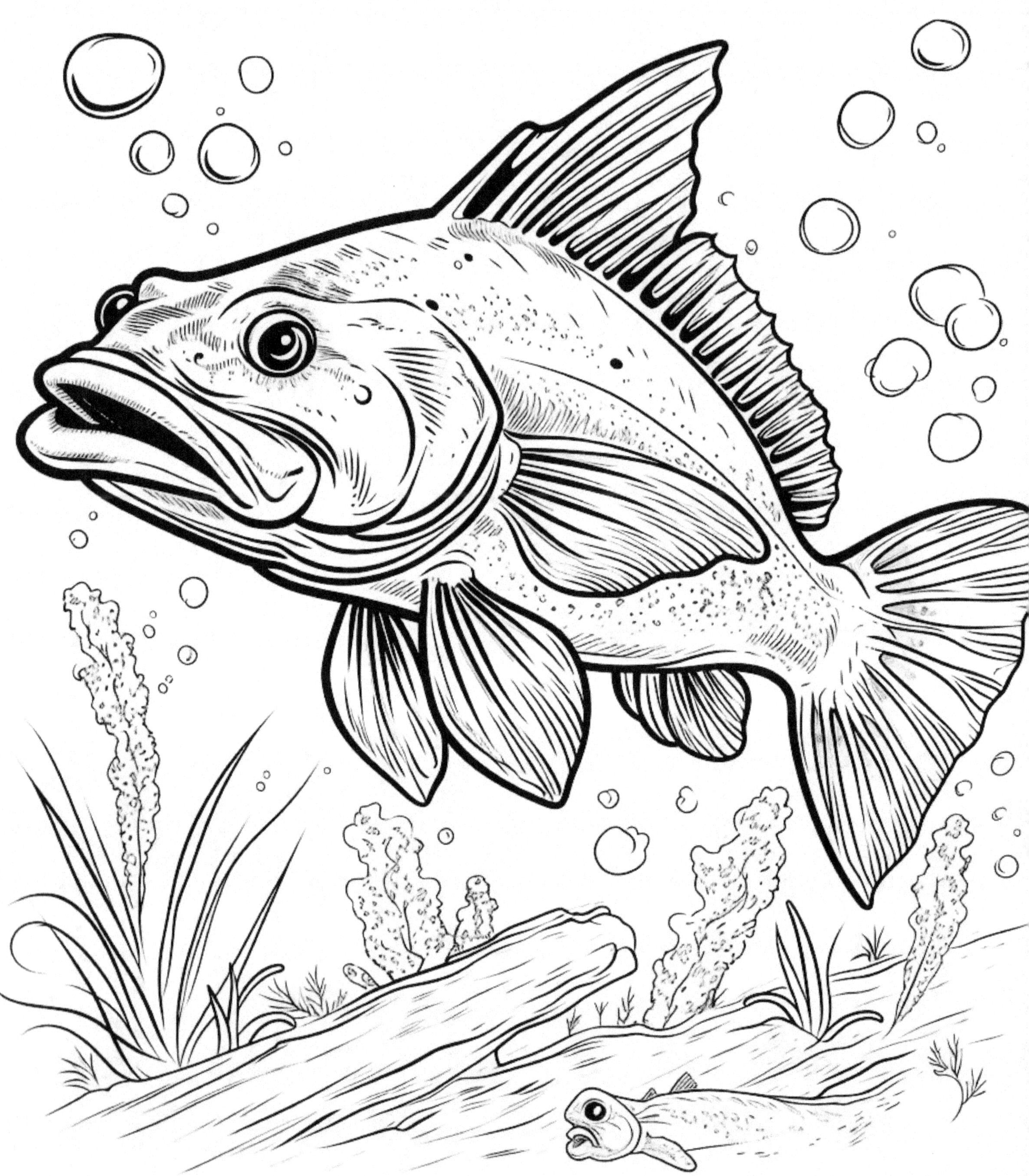

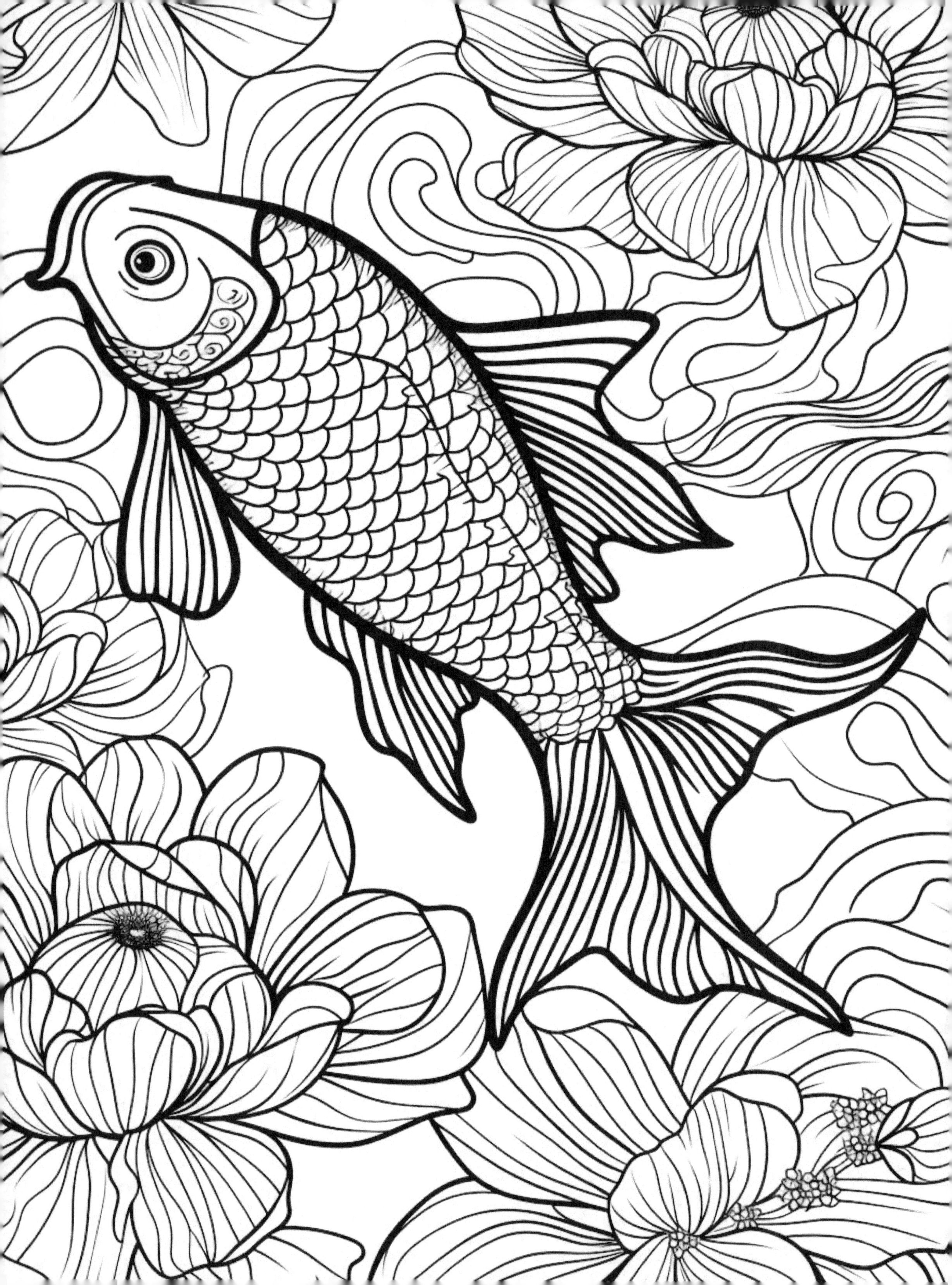

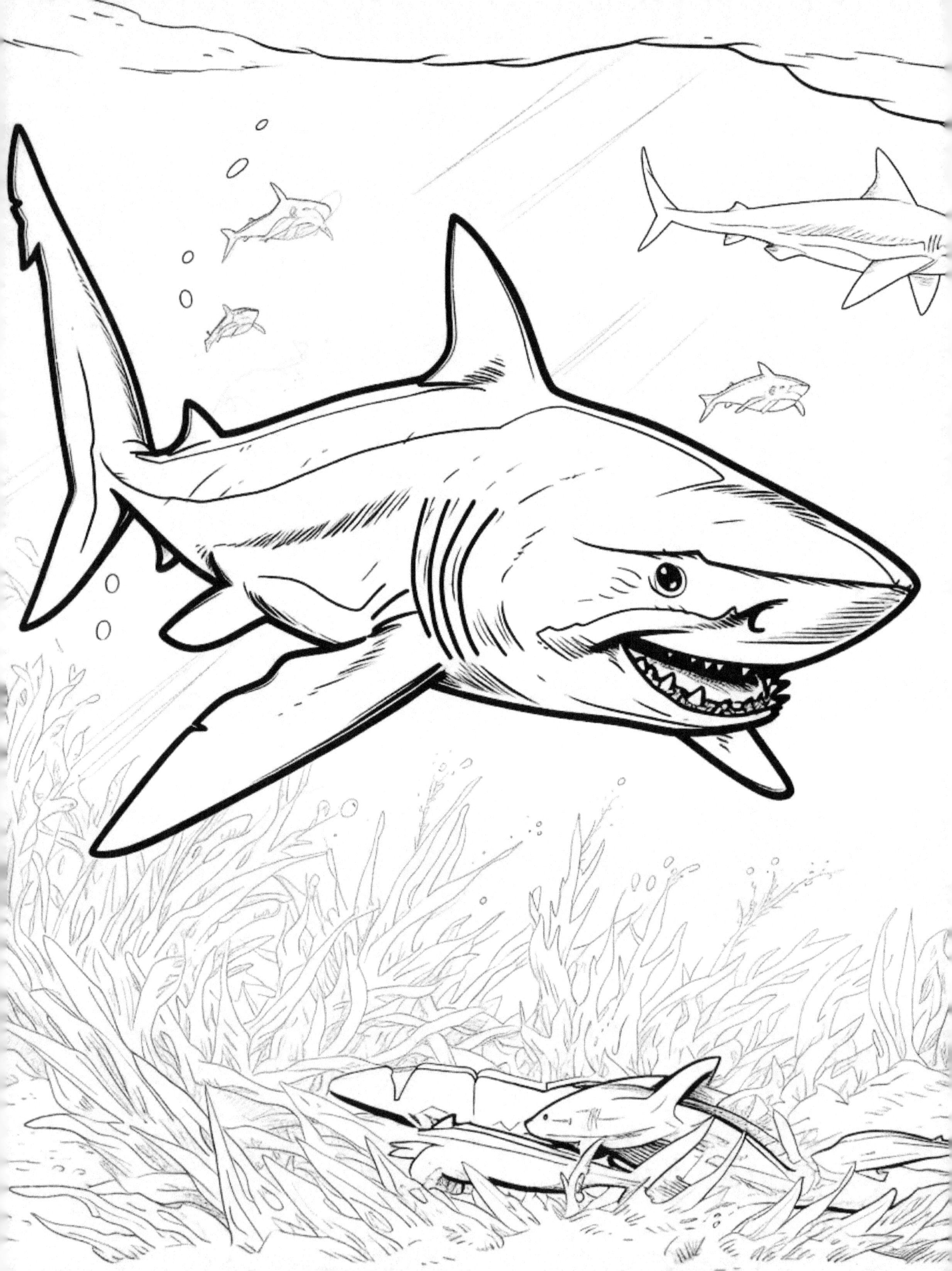

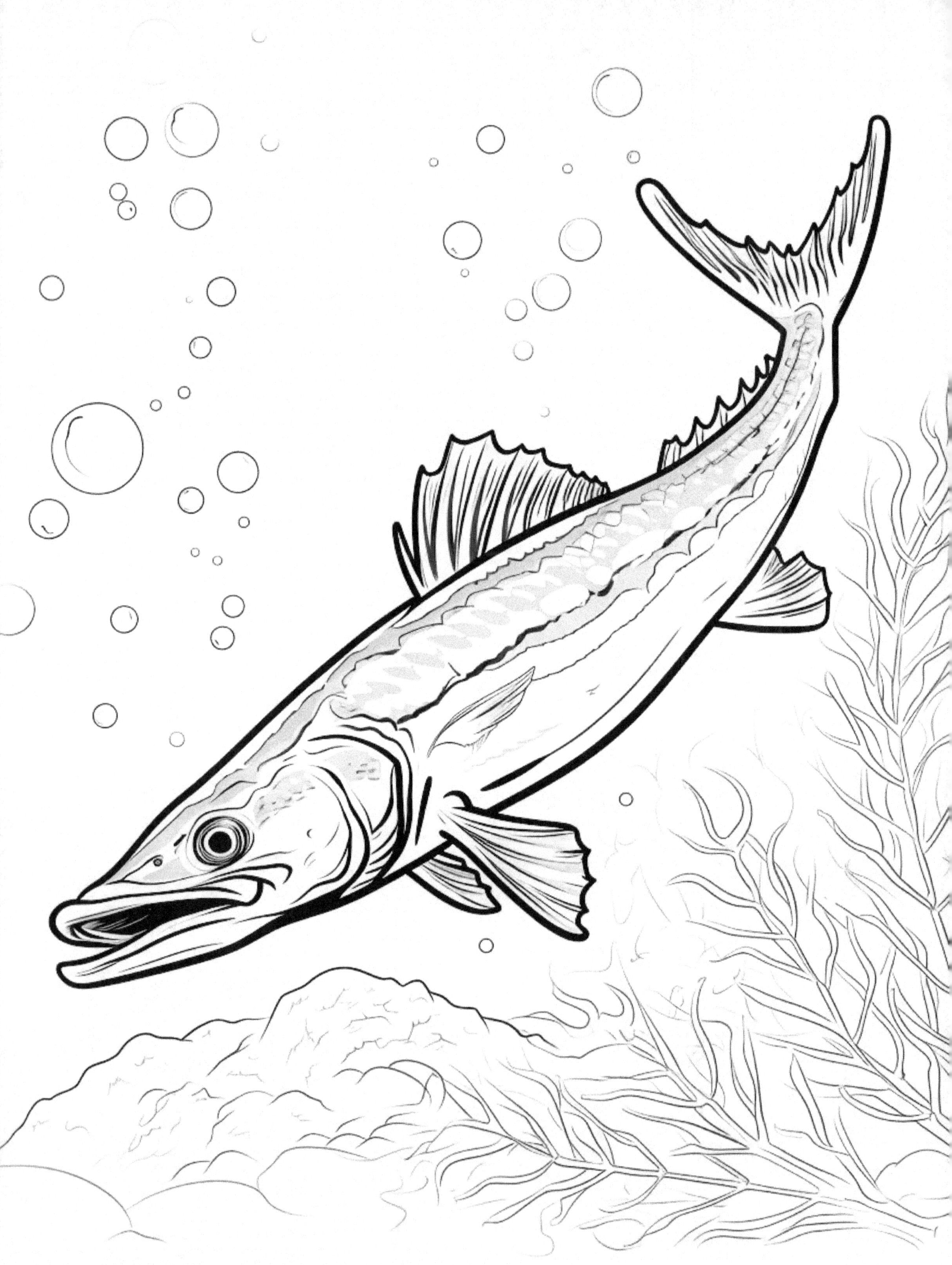

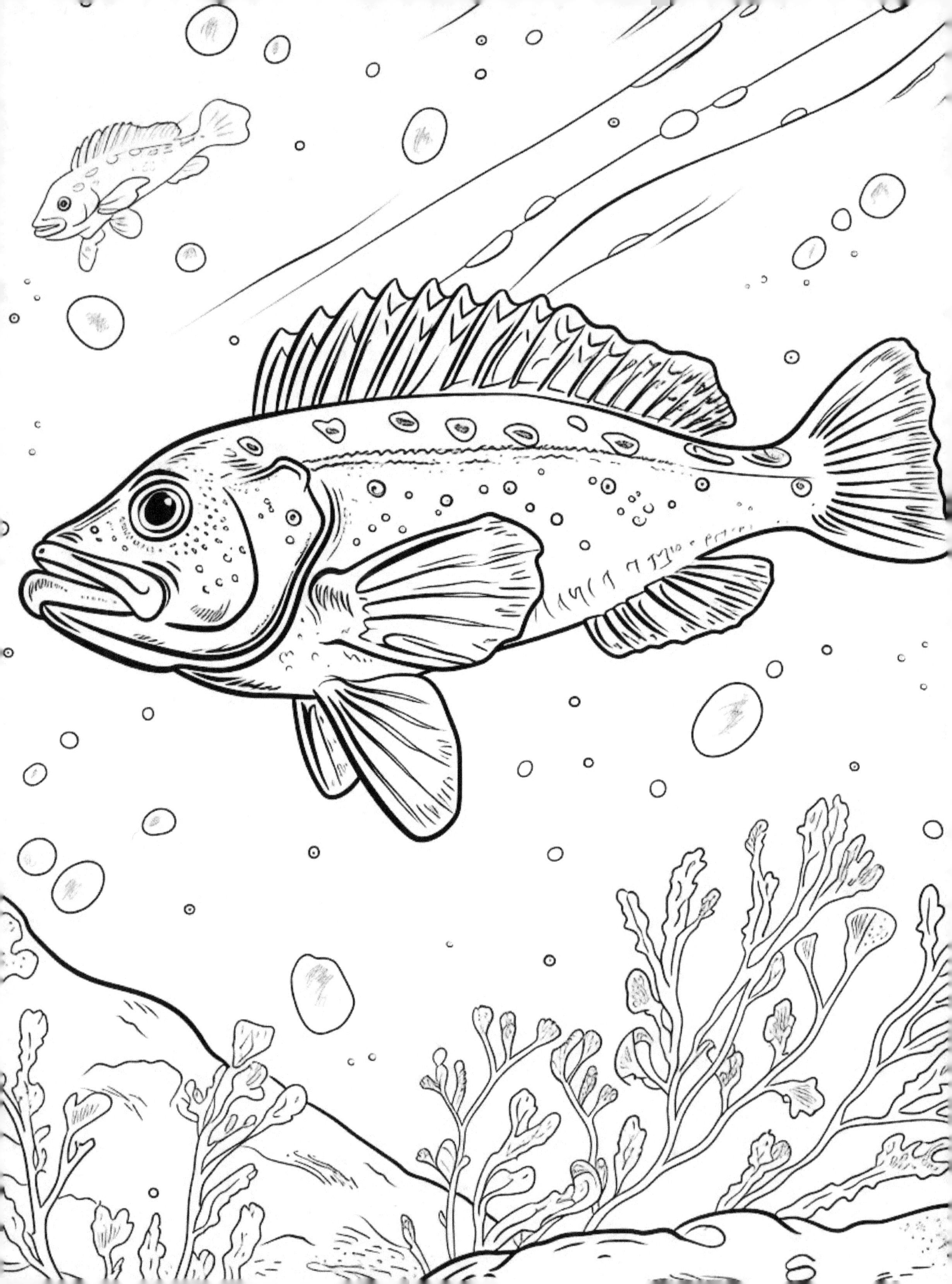

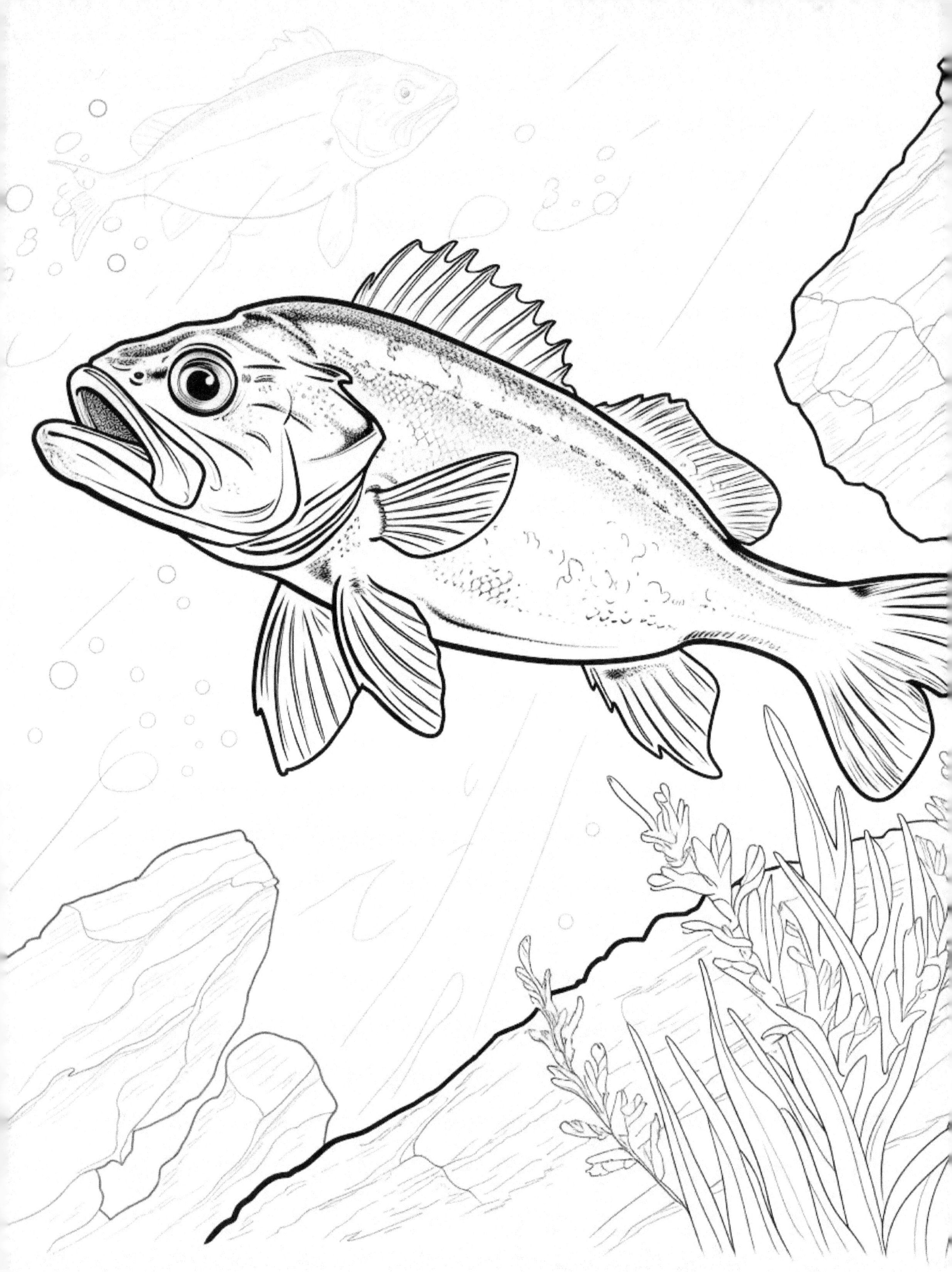

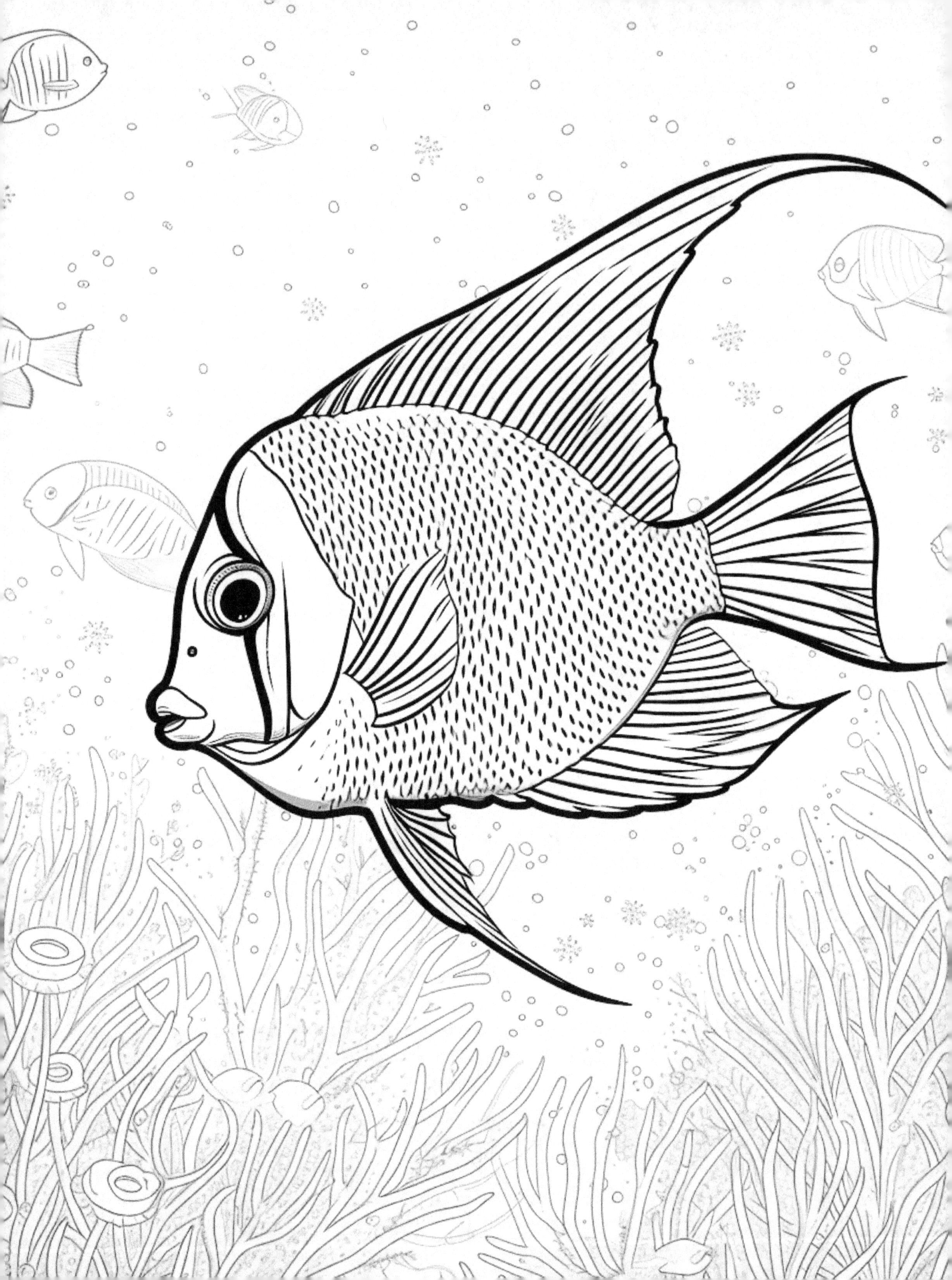

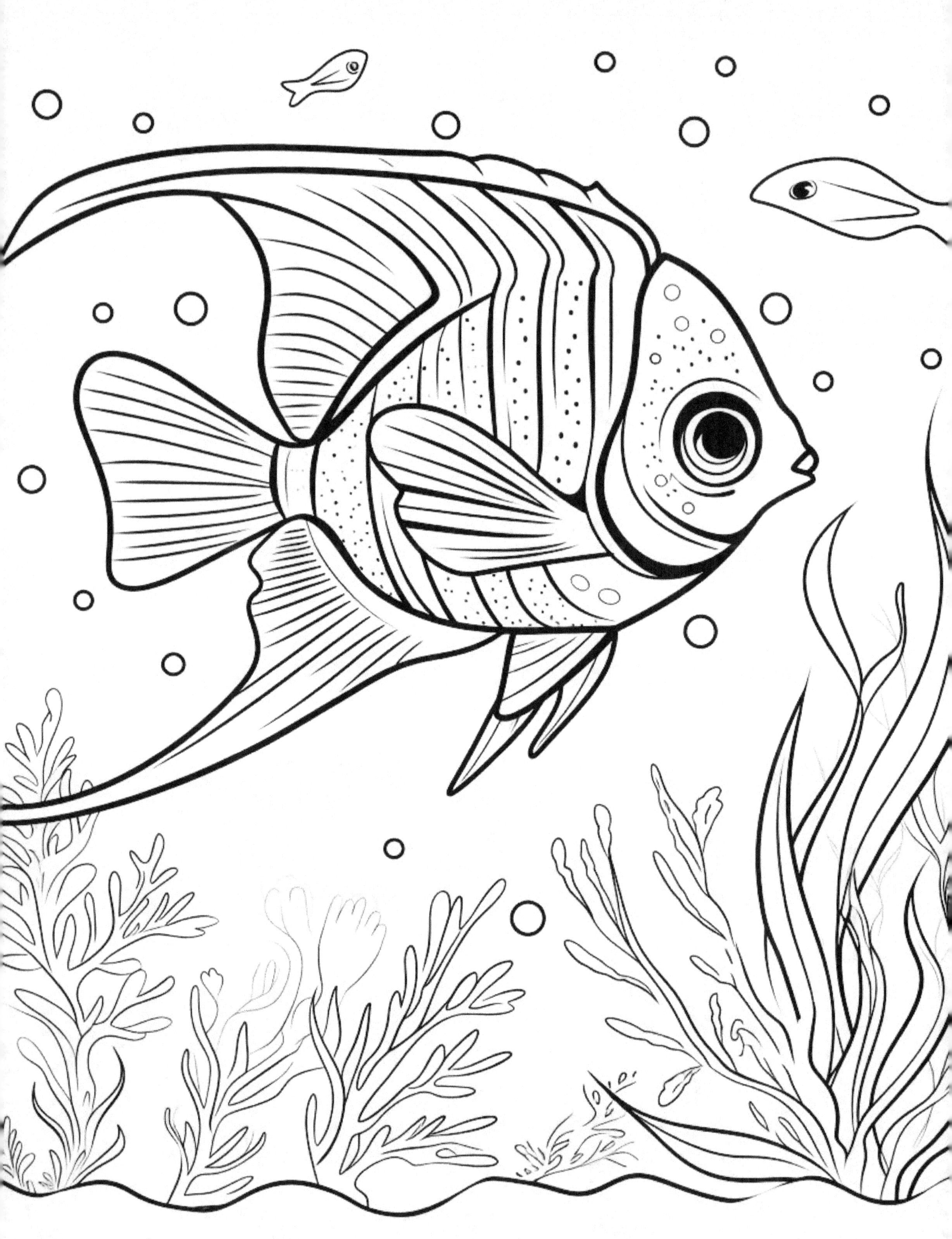

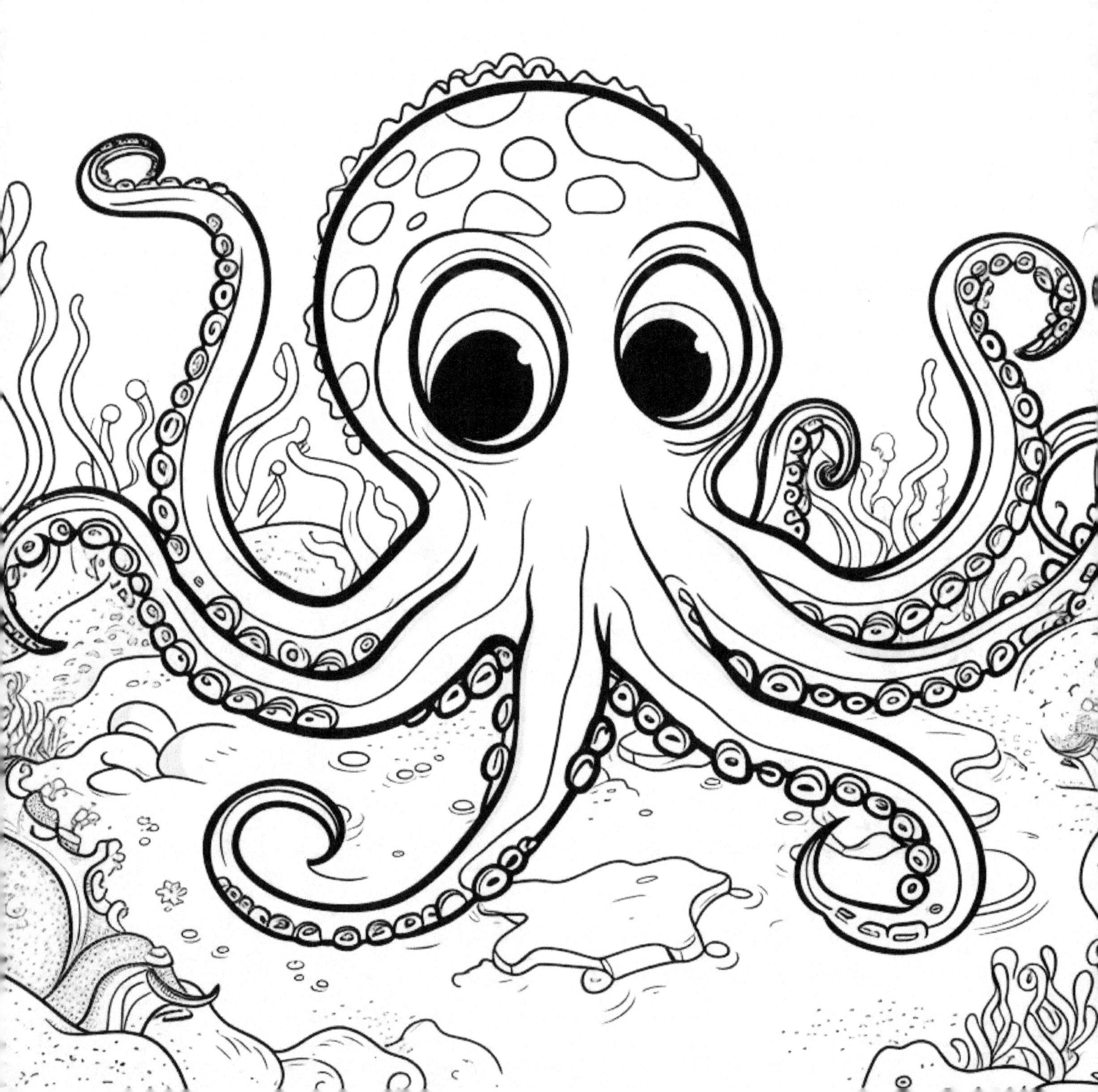

Thank you for exploring the ocean depths
with me!

I hope you've enjoyed coloring these amazing
water animals and their enchanting
backgrounds.

May your creativity continue to flow like the
ocean currents!

Remember, the ocean is full of wonder and
possibilities. Keep exploring, keep learning,
and keep coloring!

Remember to share your colorful creations
on customer reviews that book!

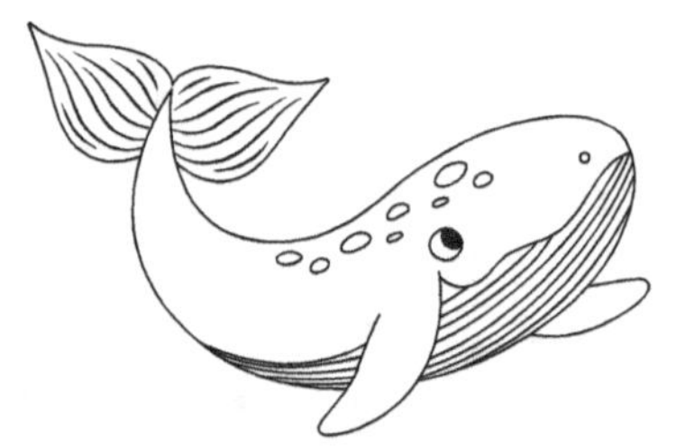

With gratitude,
Artur Sobolevskij